IMAGES
of America

SHASTA COUNTY
COPPER TOWNS

A Quartz Hill Railroad crew is shown standing on the 3.5-mile-long track between Quartz Hill and Curago. The railroad was developed to assure a steady supply of quartz flux was delivered to the Mammoth Mining Company smelter at Coram. (Courtesy of Ralph Hollibaugh.)

ON THE COVER: A group of miners are pictured at the Iron Mountain Mine with their children. (Courtesy of Ralph Hollibaugh.)

IMAGES of America

SHASTA COUNTY COPPER TOWNS

Ron Jolliff with the Shasta Historical Society

ARCADIA
PUBLISHING

Copyright © 2021 by Ron Jolliff with the Shasta Historical Society
ISBN 978-1-4671-0596-5

Published by Arcadia Publishing
Charleston, South Carolina

Printed in the United States of America

Library of Congress Control Number: 2020949324

For all general information, please contact Arcadia Publishing:
Telephone 843-853-2070
Fax 843-853-0044
E-mail sales@arcadiapublishing.com
For customer service and orders:
Toll-Free 1-888-313-2665

Visit us on the Internet at www.arcadiapublishing.com

To Diana Hollibaugh.

CONTENTS

ACKNOWLEDGMENTS

This book was a collaborative effort using the photograph collections of the Shasta Historical Society and the eclectic collection of Ralph Hollibaugh. Hollibaugh's collection is a varied assortment of all things Shasta County from Gold Rush letters, postal covers, bottles, ephemera, and photographs to Chinese opium wares. Without his view that history needs to be shared and published to make it available for further research, this book would not have been possible.

I would also acknowledge Jay Thompson for his assistance in obtaining copies from the Shasta Historical Society collection and Heather Farquhar, director, and Nancy Shaw, executive assistant, of the Shasta Historical Society for their encouragement.

I would be remiss in not thanking Arcadia Publishing for multiple reasons. I would like to point out another Images of America edition: *Shasta Lake Boomtowns and the Building of Shasta Dam* by Al Rocca, which begins where this work ends and addresses the next boom in Shasta County's history. Most importantly, I would like to thank Arcadia Publishing for providing a format that can help the younger generation enjoy the study and understanding of local history.

The author's royalties from sales of this book will be donated to the Shasta Historical Society so that it can continue its mission of preserving local history.

INTRODUCTION

Between 1896 and 1965, the mines of Shasta County, California, produced almost 704 million pounds of copper, more than half the statewide production during the same period. The West Shasta Copper-Zinc District extends along the western side of the Sacramento River from Iron Mountain to Backbone Creek, while the East Shasta Copper-Zinc District extends along the lower Pit River and south to Ingot in the Cow Creek Valley. Both districts contain massive deposits of copper sulfide ore that contains zinc, lead, silver, and gold. Although the native Wintu population obtained the uncombined form known as native copper from the Pit River, it was placer gold that first attracted Euro-American settlers.

Gold was discovered on Clear Creek in southern Shasta County in the spring of 1848 after local Mexican land grant holder Pierson B. Reading investigated Marshall's discovery at Coloma and recognized similar geologic features. Reading began mining using Native American labor, and before 1849, several hundred miners were working the "northern mines" at camps such as One Horse Town, Reading's Springs, and Whiskeytown. As the camps began to thrive, the population grew, and prospectors expanded their search to new areas such as the Sacramento Canyon and Pit River. Generally, gold was found west of the Sacramento River, centering on Spring Creek and Iron Mountain, but discoveries were also made at Squaw Creek on the Pit River and at Old Diggings (Buckeye). As placer gold deposits were being depleted, the focus turned to lode mining, which continued to operate alongside and often in conjunction with the copper companies that were to follow. The Franklin and Milkmaid began lode operations in 1852, and other mines such as the Central, Iron Mountain, Texas Consolidated, Diamond King (Copley), Evening Star, Original Quartz Hill, and Reid continued operations into the copper boom. Each mine with its ore processing mill attracted small settlements, and some, like the Texas Consolidated (Hart), grew to be represented by one of 21 post offices established across Shasta's copper districts. Nor were gold and copper the only sources of mineral wealth within the copper-zinc districts: cadmium was produced at the Mammoth group, lead was produced around Ingot, and silver at the Afterthought, Balaklala, Mammoth, Shasta King, and Golinsky Mines. With increased technology, zinc was produced at the Afterthought, Balaklala, Bully Hill, Iron Mountain, and Mammoth mines, while barite was produced at Bully Hill. Iron was prominent near the junction of the McCloud and Pit Rivers, where the Noble Electric Steel Company built an iron smelter.

Despite this diverse mineral wealth, the copper industry boomed and failed in step with mining technology. The local sulfide ore defeated early attempts at processing at Copper City and Furnaceville, but by the 1890s, the tough ore was subjected to new smelting technology, and the extension of the Southern Pacific Railroad north from Redding in 1884 made the mines more accessible. The new smelting technology used limestone and quartz as a flux, and massive outcropping of both was available in both copper-zinc districts. Soon, limestone quarries were opened at Bibben and Black Mountain near Ingot, at Doak for the Shasta Iron Company, and Holt & Gregg and the Mountain Copper Company had quarries to support smelters at Kennett,

Keswick, and Coram. It was the perfect combination of railroad access, new technology, ore with a high copper content, and locally available sources of flux, all coupled with a high demand for copper, that created a boom that lasted from the 1890s to the 1920s. For a short time, the resulting towns like Kennett were major population centers hosting assorted businesses, organizations, and entertainment to rival Redding to the south.

The caldron of wealth created by copper production also caused many to look at reality through a set of blinders. It was not hard to see the flaws, as the smelting process quickly filled the Sacramento Valley below the smelters with toxic smoke containing sulfur dioxide that destroyed crops and the prosperous fruit orchards of Cottonwood and Happy Valley. Wood harvesting for roasting ore and mine timbers denuded hillsides and soon encroached on federal holdings, leading to severe soil erosion. Fish kills were soon noted in Redding. At first, the courts' sympathies rested with the big investment companies, but slowly, the edge turned toward the farmers in what was known locally as "the Farmer-Smelter War." Farmer's organizations were grudgingly joined by federal lawsuits that slowly eroded profits and forced some attempts at modifying the smelting process before finally forcing the smelters to close. The real death knell for the smelters was the fragility of world copper prices. Dips in the market had created temporary closures before, but at the end of World War I, prices plummeted and remained low. Smelter after smelter was closed due to rising legal costs and lower returns. The larger mines continued to produce ore for shipment to distant smelters or altered production to focus on use in fertilizers or for other industrial uses.

The population of smelter towns plummeted almost as quickly as they had blossomed, but some held on as towns like Kennett were transportation hubs and others were supported by a drastically reduced mining industry. The realization that the end was near came when the California legislature authorized the Mid-Pacific Region California Central Valley Project in 1933. The act called for the sale of revenue bonds to resolve water problems, but it was in the midst of the Great Depression when no one was buying, so in 1935, the federal government took control with the Rivers and Harbors Act. In 1937, the Bureau of Reclamation took over the Central Valley Project with the aim of improving flood control, providing water for irrigation, and generating electric power. The construction of Shasta Dam began in 1938 as the key facility in the project. The 602-foot-high concrete gravity dam was completed in 1945. As water began to be stored, Kennett, Copper City, and all but a few structures at Bully Hill were submerged under the new Lake Shasta. The rising water necessitated the construction of a new Pit River Bridge and the rerouting of the highway and railroad, thus cutting off sites below the dam. Over a million check dams and millions of trees were planted below the dam and around the new lake to stop erosion on the denuded hillsides.

The clean-up efforts to neutralize some of the effects of copper mining continue today at the Environmental Protection Agency's Iron Mountain Superfund site and five other sites in the copper-zinc district, but these are generally out of sight of the public drawn to Lake Shasta for its recreational resources. Few of the visitors to the lake realize the wealth of mining and railroad history, not to mention personal histories, that lay near the lake or below its surface. Hopefully, this book will draw attention to the thousands who were born, raised, and worked in Shasta County's copper towns.

One

Bully Hill to Pitt
East Shasta Copper-Zinc District

The settlements at Squaw Creek began in the early 1850s after placer gold was discovered, but it was not until the mid-1860s that lode mining began in conjunction with the boom at Copper City. The operations surrounding the Bully Hill Mine were small until 1877, when the Extra Mining Company built a mill at Copper City to process gold and silver ore from Bully Hill. Development dwindled when sulfide ore was reached, as the milling process was inadequate to extract the precious metals. With new developments in smelting technology, James Sallee next developed properties at Squaw Creek aiming at the copper potential. The small community of Salee takes its name from this period. In 1899, Capt. Joseph Raphael De Lamar purchased 18 claims from Sallee.

In 1900, De Lamar established a smelter with a 150-ton-per-day capacity. The new town of Delamar grew up near the smelter, about a mile and a half below the mine. De Lamar constructed a railroad to connect the Bully Hill Mine to the smelter at Winthrop, which became known as the Delamar Railroad.

In 1900, the post office was established at the headquarters of De Lamar's projects at Winthrop and took the same name for the Winthrop Mining claim that De Lamar had purchased in 1899. The area at Winthrop where the managerial staff had their bungalows became known as Circle City.

De Lamar formed the Bully Hill Copper Mining and Smelting Company, but the new company faced one major frustration: transportation. Freight and processed copper had to be moved by wagon over the mountains to a railhead. Capt. De Lamar sold the company in 1905 to General Electric Company of New York when copper prices were in a steady rise. To alleviate the transportation problem, General Electric looked for a more direct railroad line. In 1907, grading commenced from the Southern Pacific siding near the junction of the Pit and Sacramento Rivers, along the Pit River, and connected to the already established Delamar Railroad. The resulting Sacramento Valley & Eastern Railroad was in operation late in 1907, connecting Pitt, Heroult, Copper City, Salee, Delamar, Winthrop, and the Bully Hill Mine to the Southern Pacific Railroad and beyond.

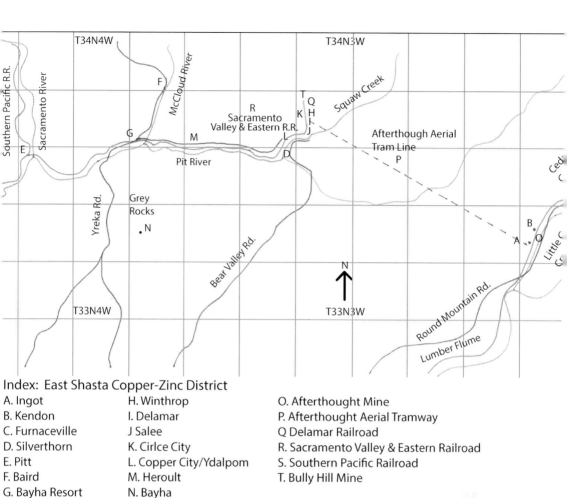

Index: East Shasta Copper-Zinc District

Although geologically connected, the East and West Shasta Copper-Zinc Districts developed separately due to transportation issues. Copper City and the mines along Squaw Creek used a route to the Cow Creek Valley before connecting with the Southern Pacific Railroad at Anderson on the Sacramento River. The separation ended with the construction of the Sacramento Valley & Eastern Railroad in 1907. (Courtesy of Andrew Jolliff.)

The Bully Hill Mine, shown here, had been worked along with several other surrounding properties since the early 1860s, but due to the difficulty of shipping and processing the ore, production remained small. After J.R. De Lamar purchased the property and settled a disputed title claim, the mine blossomed with the establishment of a smelter at Winthrop. (Courtesy of Ralph Hollibaugh.)

This photograph is looking from the Bully Hill Mine toward the smelter and Pit River. The operations surrounding the Bully Hill Mine were small until 1877, when the Extra Mining Company built a mill at Copper City to process ore from Bully Hill. The company extracted $640,000 in silver and gold from the surface ores, but development dwindled when sulfide ore was reached, as the milling process was inadequate to release the precious metals. James Sallee, who, along with Magee and Camden, had sold the Iron Mountain Mine to the Mountain Copper Company, started developing properties at Squaw Creek. The small community of Salee takes its name from this period. In 1899, Capt. Joseph Raphael De Lamar purchased 18 claims from Sallee. (Courtesy of Ralph Hollibaugh.)

In all, the Bully Hill Mine had six entrance tunnels that served 11 levels within the mine. The main shaft was about 800 feet deep. This picture shows a catch basin and runoff from the Bully Hill Mine that ran into Squaw Creek. (Courtesy of Ralph Hollibaugh.)

In 1899, Captain De Lamar built a narrow-gauge railroad (30 inches between the inner edges of the track) to haul ore 1.5 miles from level 3 of the Bully Hill Mine to the smelter at Winthrop. The Delamar Railroad, as it was called, utilized the diminutive Shay steam locomotive shown here. In 1908, the Delamar Railroad became a portion of the Sacramento Valley & Eastern Railroad, which used standard gauge (4 feet, 8.5 inches between the rails). (Courtesy of Ralph Hollibaugh.)

A hoist, or winder, was used in a mine to raise or lower conveyances within the mine shaft. The hoist shown here, at the 1,200-foot elevation of the Bully Hill Mine, is a double-drum hoist where the cable is wound around the drum. The double drum allowed the hoisting of two conveyances in balance (one lifted and one lowered). The cable was run through a head frame out of view to the top and served an 800-foot-deep shaft. (Courtesy of Ralph Hollibaugh.)

This photograph shows miners loading an ore cart at the Bully Hill Mine. The orebodies ranged up to 300 feet in length and width and up to 40 feet in thickness. (Courtesy of Shasta Historical Society.)

13

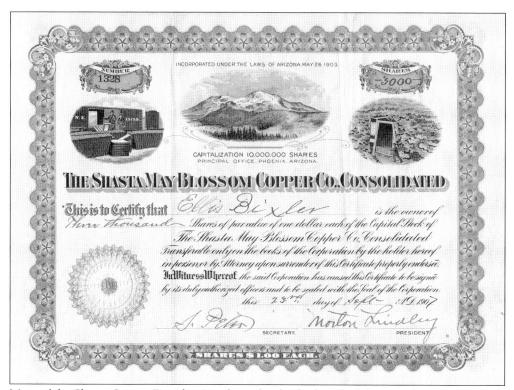

Maps of the Shasta Copper-Zinc districts showed a checkerboard of claims and companies, with many of the smaller companies having a symbiotic relationship that benefited them by utilizing the smelters operated by the larger companies. This 1907 stock certificate is for the Shasta May Blossom Copper Company, which operated the Keith group of claims just 800 feet from the Bully Hill Mine. The company had been reorganized in 1903 from the Shasta May Blossom Mining and Smelting Company. In 1916, the company was reported to have only two men employed at the mine. (Courtesy of Ralph Hollibaugh.)

In 1899, Captain De Lamar purchased the Winthrop claim shown here and in 1900 located his smelter on the site. In 1900, the Winthrop Post Office was opened, taking the name of the claim. Smelting operations ceased in 1927, but the post office remained open until 1932, when services were moved down Squaw Creek to the Ydalpom Post Office. (Courtesy of Ralph Hollibaugh.)

This postcard shows De Lamar's smelter at Winthrop, with roasting ovens to the left and a footbridge to town in the foreground. In 1900, De Lamar established a smelter with a 150-ton-per-day capacity. The smelter ran roasted ore through a furnace, and then the furnace matte was processed in a convertor to blister copper. The ingots of blister copper were then shipped to another De Lamar plant in New Jersey for further processing. In 1906–1907, the smelter was enlarged to process 400 tons of ore per day. De Lamar constructed a railroad to connect the Bully Hill Mine to the smelter at Delamar, which became known as the Delamar Railroad. (Courtesy of Ralph Hollibaugh.)

Roasting stalls at Bully Hill smelter, shown here, are where ore was treated before being put in the furnace. Ore statistics for the Bully Hill–Rising Star for the period 1900 to 1950 totaled 48.8 million pounds of copper, 25.1 million pounds of zinc, 38,000 ounces of gold, and 2.2 million ounces of silver. (Courtesy of Shasta Historical Society.)

In 1917, the Bully Hill Mining Company was acquired by Walter Arnstein and his associates. Along with the Bully Hill Mine, the company acquired the nearby Rising Star Mine. Ore from the mines was initially shipped to Kennett for smelting until the discovery of high-grade zinc ore (up to 20 percent zinc) at the Rising Star Mine. In 1918, Arnstein constructed the flotation mill seen here in 1920 around the old smelter at Winthrop, and smelting operations revived. Shasta Zinc consolidated several more mines, including the Afterthought at Ingot, and built an aerial tramway from Ingot to deliver the ore in 1925. The smelter suffered a shutdown in 1922 due to falling copper prices, and the company passed to the Glidden Company. All operations ceased at the mill in 1927. (Courtesy of Shasta Historical Society.)

The history of the Rising Star Mine, shown in this photograph, was identical to that of the Bully Hill Mine. In the 1860s, the upper levels of gossans or ores that were oxidized by weathering and leaching were worked for gold and silver. The mine was again active in 1877 when it was worked by the Extra Mining Company again for gold and silver. The mine is only 1,600 feet from the Bully Hill Mine and the workings of the mine approached within 500 feet of the Bully Hill Mine. The mine was active for copper when James Sallee developed Squaw Creek but was not purchased by Captain De Lamar. (Courtesy of Ralph Hollibaugh.)

Drilling technology had to keep pace with other technological advancements in mining. Here, a crew in the Rising Star Mine is using a larger bore Burley Drill that is braced against the ceiling. The Burley was an improvement on percussive or hammer drills and could drill deeper to meet the requirements for blasting with dynamite. (Courtesy of Ralph Hollibaugh.)

This image shows an ore train leaving the Rising Star Mine pulled by a two-horse team. The main shaft of the Rising Star was about 750 feet deep, and the ore was divided into three main bodies. One of the ore bodies was high in sphalerite (zinc-iron sulfide), the main ore of zinc (up to 20 percent) that drew the attention of Walter Arnstein, president of the Oakland and Antioch Railroad and owner of the Nevada County Narrow Gauge Railroad. Arnstein acquired both the Rising Star and Bully Hill Mines and built a zinc plant at Winthrop. (Courtesy of Ralph Hollibaugh.)

This postcard shows Main Street in Delamar, but the town name was also given as DeLaMar and DeLamar. A substantial section of the town burned in 1902, and much of the business district burned again in 1910. The shoreline of Lake Shasta now extends across this area of Main Street. (Courtesy of Ralph Hollibaugh.)

This photograph shows the Fourth of July parade down the Main Street of Delamar. In 1870, the US Congress made the Fourth of July an unpaid holiday for federal workers. By 1900, there were seven federally recognized holidays: Christmas, New Years, Independence Day, Thanksgiving, Decoration Day (now Memorial Day), and Labor Day. Independence Day in all the mines and communities was a time for parades, fireworks (often dynamite), picnics, and baseball. (Courtesy of Shasta Historical Society.)

The saloon in this photograph has its location given as Bully Hill in the early 1900s, so it was most likely in Delamar. The mirror behind the bar has "Happy New Year" written on it. (Courtesy of Shasta Historical Society.)

This image shows the students and teachers at the Delamar School in 1906. When the Bully Hill smelter and Mine were in operation, there were about 2,000 employees, and the population of Delamar greatly exceeded that number. The school district also supported not only Delamar but nearby communities such as Salee and Winthrop. (Courtesy of Shasta Historical Society.)

Circle City, shown here, is where the management of the Bully Hill Mine and smelter lived. Couples resided in the bungalows, while bachelors lived in the big building. (Courtesy of Ralph Hollibaugh.)

Engineer Lawrence May from the Bully Hill smelter and his wife, Florence Mesing, are enjoying a picnic around 1910. The child at center is Elsie J. May, who was born in Winthrop in 1908. Lawrence May was typical of mining engineers of the time, moving from mining operation to mining operation and, often, from country to country, as many of the largest mining firms had international holdings. He worked in Mexico prior to coming to Bully Hill and in Cuba after leaving. (Courtesy of Ralph Hollibaugh.)

This photograph is of a domestic servant at Circle City. The management staff at Circle City employed nannies, cooks, and gardeners and lived in a cultured environment far apart from the miners and other workers. (Courtesy of Ralph Hollibaugh.)

Common laborers, shown here at Circle City bringing wood and kindling, were often newly arrived immigrants, especially from Italy and to a lesser degree from other areas of southern Europe, such as Greece and Portugal. (Courtesy of Ralph Hollibaugh.)

The community of Circle City was a bastion of aristocracy set off from its working-class neighbors and complete with a full domestic staff of cooks, nannies, and gardeners. For some, such as this Chinese cook, life was not enlivened with picnics, hunting parties, and parlor games. In 1900, after Chinese cooks passed through Redding on their way to the mines, the citizens of Copper City, Salee, and Delamar held a mass meeting attempting to bar their employment. Two Chinese cooks were physically removed from the stage and forced to leave the county. Shasta County remained a hotbed of anti-Oriental labor sentiment throughout the copper boom. (Courtesy of Ralph Hollibaugh.)

Much of the land surrounding both copper-zinc districts was under federal control, and the relationship between the mine owners and the government was often strained by legal suits over illegal wood harvesting and damage caused by sulfur dioxide fumes. After the election of Theodore Roosevelt and his enactment of conservation programs, both sides cooperated to bring the herd of 51 elk, shown here from Wyoming by train to Bully Hill for release in 1911. Offspring of the federal release can still be seen on the Pit arm of Lake Shasta. (Courtesy of Ralph Hollibaugh.)

The Copper City Post Office and general store is seen here around 1900. Copper City was into its third mining boom when the post office was established in 1878, but shortly afterward, the mines encountered sulfide ores that resisted free milling. Faced with having to ship ore to Wales for processing, the boom ended. The post office was closed in 1880, and operations moved to Redding. When the post office returned to Copper City in 1888, it took a different name: Ydalpom. The new name caused some confusion, as the address was written "Copper City, Ydalpom Post Office." The name Ydalpom means "north-lying place" in local Wintu. The post office stayed open until 1943, when Lake Shasta was beginning to flood Squaw Creek. (Courtesy of Shasta Historical Society.)

A ferry was established across the Pit River, about a mile above Squaw Creek, in 1853 that connected traffic from the Cow Creek area via Bear Valley (now Jones Valley) to placer diggings along the Pit River. In 1853, the license for the ferry was issued to Hughes, Silverthorne, and Berryhill, but by 1854, it had passed solely to George W. Silverthorne. He and his Yurok wife, Lucy, built the first cabin, and a small settlement followed. The site, along with Baird, became a gathering place for local Wintu. During the period from 1901 to 1907, freight and smelter production from Bully Hill were hauled by wagon across the ferry and on to the railhead of the Anderson & Bella Vista Railroad. The small community shown in this photograph lasted until 1944, when water from Shasta Lake inundated the site. (Courtesy of Shasta Historical Society.)

This is an overview of Copper City showing the road to Bully Hill at center. Copper City was near the junction of the Pit River and Squaw Creek. (Courtesy of Shasta Historical Society.)

STREET SCENE IN Copper City

This is an early street scene at Copper City prior to 1906, when the Sacramento Valley & Eastern Railroad laid railroad tracks down the center of the street. The town of Copper City had a long and varied mining history that covered four boom periods. The first rush occurred in 1852 when Capt. O.R. Johnson discovered gold. As the placer deposits were quickly worked, the boom quieted but never fully died. The resulting Pittsburg Mining District continued being worked by a small population of miners. In 1862, Swedish miner Charles Williams discovered ore rich in silver and started the second boom. At the time, copper was also mined, but the profits were marginal, as the ore had to be shipped to Wales for smelting. By 1866, the second boom was over. The third boom began in 1877, when the Extra Mining Company built a mill at Copper City extracting mainly silver and gold. The boom dwindled after sulfide ores were reached in the local mines, as the precious metals could not be recovered by free milling, and the expense of shipping the ore to distant smelters was prohibitive. (Courtesy of Shasta Historical Society.)

Ira Engle, the owner of the Copper City Mercantile, is seen standing next to a railroad car in 1921. With level ground at a premium, the Sacramento Valley & Eastern Railroad not only laid its tracks across the yard of the Copper City School, but also down Main Street. (Courtesy of Shasta Historical Society.)

The unissued stock certificate shown here is for the Ophir Gold, Silver, and Copper Mining Company dated 1864. The company was owned by the W.H. Fender & Company. William Fender operated a chair and furniture company powered by water from Cow Creek. He was the son of Aaron Fender, who founded the Shasta Coal Mining Company in 1875. By 1865, the boom around Copper City was fading, and most work on the mine ceased when the ore proved resistant to recovering the precious metals. (Courtesy of Ralph Hollibaugh.)

The Copper City School was reached by the footbridge across Squaw Creek seen here. The school district experienced the same boom-and-bust history as the local mines. The district was founded in 1864, only to be closed in 1867. It was reestablished in 1878, but by 1880 saw a declining population. After the establishment of the Bully Hill smelter, the district again blossomed for two decades. (Courtesy of Ralph Hollibaugh.)

This image shows Earl Sholes and his class at the Copper City School. Sholes served in the Medical Corps during World War I and died in the line of duty in 1950 as undersheriff of Shasta County. (Courtesy of Ralph Hollibaugh.)

27

The Copper City Mercantile Company served Copper City during its final decades. Copper City was earlier known as Brownsville, then Williams. From 1864 to 1866, the town was of sufficient size to support a newspaper, the *Copper City Pioneer*. (Courtesy of Ralph Hollibaugh.)

Much of the ore processed at Copper City by the Extra Mining Company after 1877 was brought in by wagon from the Bully Hill Mine. The ore was delivered to the ore bins shown here at Copper City. (Courtesy of Ralph Hollibaugh.)

Heroult is seen here, with the Pit River in the foreground. Heroult was not a copper mining town but is included as it was a depot for the Sacramento Valley & Eastern Railroad, and its development stems from the Keswick Electric Company, founded by H.H. Noble and Lord Keswick. The Keswick Electric Company was one of the predecessors of the Northern California Power Company (later Pacific Gas & Electric Company) that provided electric power to both copper districts. (Courtesy of Ralph Hollibaugh.)

This stock certificate for the Noble Electric Steel Company is incorrectly dated August 1901 and signed by H.H. Noble. The company was founded in July 1907 by Hamden Holmes Noble, who in 1899 formed the Keswick Electric Company with Lord Keswick. The company constructed a smelter at Heroult to process ore by use of electricity. In 1919, the company was forced into receivership and by 1924 was taken over by the Shasta Iron & Steel Company. (Courtesy of Ralph Hollibaugh.)

This three-story boardinghouse was built for the smelter workers at Heroult. Boardinghouses were a staple of all mining towns, as the majority of employees were young, single, lacking resources, and transient due to the frequent opening and closing of mines and smelters. (Courtesy of Shasta Historical Society.)

The Heroult smelter was founded in 1907 by the Noble Electric Steel Company. The smelter used an electric arc process on locally mined iron ore. The post office at Heroult was also founded in 1907, and both were named for Dr. Paul Heroult, a French metallurgist who sold H.H. Noble the patent and helped install the smelter. The smelter closed in 1919, but the post office remained open until 1928, when operations were moved to Baird on the McCloud River. (Courtesy of Ralph Hollibaugh.)

This photograph shows the Heroult smelter in 1912. The town established a school district in 1916 that remained in operation until 1927. (Courtesy of Shasta Historical Society.)

The Sacramento Valley & Eastern Railroad siding at the Heroult smelter was used to move iron ore to the smelter. After the smelter closed, the Shasta Iron Company continued producing iron ore after the surrender of the Noble lease. Ten to fifteen railcars of iron ore were shipped per month until the mine became idle at the end of the 1920s. (Courtesy of Shasta Historical Society.)

Molten pig iron is being poured at the Heroult smelter. The process, invented by Paul Heroult, was discovered at the same time by American Charles Martin Hall, and the Hall-Heroult process remains the predominant smelting technique used worldwide for aluminum production. (Courtesy of Shasta Historical Society.)

Local teachers Kate Smith (right) and Carrie Keith ride an ore cart from the company iron mine to Heroult. The Shasta Iron Company first began iron production of high-grade magnetite in 1892 before the mine was leased to the Noble Electric Steel Company. From 1942 to 1946, Carrico and Gautier leased the Shasta Iron Company mine, but because of the rising waters of Lake Shasta, the ore could not be shipped via Heroult but had to be ferried across the McCloud arm. The ore was taken over the new Pit River Bridge to Redding, where it was crushed, screened, and washed. (Courtesy of Shasta Historical Society.)

This photograph shows the dirt road near Heroult with the bridge at the junction of the McCloud and Pit Rivers in the background. Just below the road are the tracks of the Sacramento Valley & Eastern Railroad. (Courtesy of Shasta Historical Society.)

A Sacramento Valley & Eastern Railroad motorcar travels along the Pitt River, going toward Bully Hill. In 1908, the railroad was opened to public use, and after the Bully Hill smelter closed in 1910, it continued operations with a "skunk" gasoline motor car to carry passengers, milk, farm equipment, papers, hay, and other everyday needs of the surviving communities. (Courtesy of Ralph Hollibaugh.)

After the General Electric Company purchased the Bully Hill Mining and Smelting Company in 1905, it solved the problem of transporting blister copper ingots over the mountains to the Anderson & Bella Vista Railroad by building the Sacramento Valley & Eastern (SV&E) Railroad in 1907. The track connected the Delamar Railroad on Squaw Creek to the Southern Pacific Railroad tracks along the west bank of the Sacramento River. The pictured SV&E engine appears to be at Pitt, the small Southern Pacific siding and community named for Robert Pitt, who provided the right-of-way, rather than for the adjacent Pit River, along which much of the SV&E operated. The small community was also known as Bonita Station and lasted until 1942, when the railroad was rerouted. The engine is pulling a Southern Pacific freight car probably loaded with supplies for the mines and towns of the East Shasta Copper-Zinc District. (Courtesy of Ralph Hollibaugh.)

This flatcar was used to haul freight and overflow passengers on the Sacramento Valley & Eastern Railroad after 1910. The attempt to recoup construction costs by opening the line to the public had limited success, but the SV&E quickly became the vital lifeblood of the local communities along the Pit River and Squaw Creek. The SV&E Railroad was totally abandoned after the flood of 1939 that destroyed the Sacramento Bridge just east of Pitt. (Courtesy of Ralph Hollibaugh.)

Railroad operations were not always smooth, as this derailment in Delamar shows. Many of the derailments were caused by erosion facilitated by sulfur dioxide released in the smelting process that killed the protective vegetation. Even the larger lines like the Southern Pacific were severely hampered by washouts, tunnel cave-ins, and derailments caused by erosion in the steep Sacramento Canyon. (Courtesy of Ralph Hollibaugh.)

The caption on this photograph states that it shows a leased Southern Pacific engine in 1919 carrying 20 individuals to Bully Hill. The need for the larger engine on the SV&E line coincided with the transition of the closed Bully Hill smelter from processing primarily copper to concentrating on zinc production. By 1920, the Bully Hill smelter was again in full production. (Courtesy of Shasta Historical Society.)

Two

INGOT-FURNACEVILLE
EAST SHASTA COPPER-ZINC DISTRICT

The second and somewhat detached section of the East Shasta Copper-Zinc District extended south of the Pit River into the Cow Creek Valley. Seven claims of the Copper Hill Group were mined for silver and gold in 1862, but the characteristics of the ore made it hard to extract the precious metals. In 1873, Marcus H. Peck purchased the Copper Hill Group, and in 1876 discovered high-grade copper ore in an adjoining lode and named it the Afterthought Mine. Peck built a reverberatory furnace and a water-jacketed furnace along North Cow Creek with access to the Reid Toll Road. The community that built up around the furnaces became known as Furnaceville. As the Afterthought Mine increased in importance, Peck built a new furnace a mile lower on Cow Creek in what had been known as Silverton and later became Ingot. As the Afterthought Mine was developed, Ingot became the primary center of business for the district.

The Afterthought Mine faced the same transportation problem that affected the Bully Hill Mine in that processed copper had to be moved 15.6 miles down a narrow valley to reach a railroad. The utilization of the Anderson–Bella Vista Railroad (Terry Railroad) was not ideal, as it was a privately owned lumber railroad that connected to the Southern Pacific at Anderson after being ferried across the Sacramento River. After the Great Western Company opened a smelter at Ingot in 1905, there was an attempt to create the Redding, Afterthought & Northeastern Railroad, without success. After a railroad bridge replaced the Sacramento River ferry, the Anderson–Bella Vista Railroad was purchased by the Afterthought Copper Company and renamed the California, Shasta & Eastern Railroad in 1913. Ore was moved from the Afterthought Mine to the smelter at Ingot using a single locomotive pulling 20 five-ton ore cars. A plan was devised to connect the rail line to Bella Vista but never materialized, as the smelter closed. The Afterthought Copper Company ceased operations in 1920. The mine had a reprieve in 1924 when the California Zinc Company took over operations and built an aerial tramway to Winthrop to process the ore at the Bully Hill smelter. By 1927, all was quiet again, although the Afterthought Mine was periodically opened for short periods into the 1950s.

This is a view of the Afterthought Mine at Ingot. The mine was initially known as the Peck Mine and had 17,200 feet of drifts and crosscuts on 11 levels with 2,200 feet of shafts, the longest being 729 feet deep. (Courtesy of Ralph Hollibaugh.)

In 1903, the Great Western Gold Company acquired the Afterthought Mine and built a smelter in 1905. In 1909, the property was acquired by the Afterthought Copper Company, which installed a reverberatory furnace and oil flotation plant. This stock certificate of the Afterthought Copper Company was issued in 1916 when there were concerns about the brokerage company managing the stock. In 1924, the property was acquired by the California Zinc Company, which built an eight-mile aerial tram to the smelter at Bully Hill that operated until 1927. (Courtesy of Ralph Hollibaugh.)

The Afterthought Mine at Ingot is seen here. During its 81.5 months of operation between 1905 and 1952, a total of 166,424 tons of ore were extracted from the mine that contained 3.23 percent copper, 16.15 percent zinc, 2.17 percent lead, 5.55 ounces of silver per ton, and 0.03 ounces of gold per ton. (Courtesy of Ralph Hollibaugh.)

The Great Western Gold Company acquired the Afterthought Mine in 1903 and operated it until 1908. The structure in the foreground is part of the 32-mile-long Terry lumber flume. (Courtesy of Ralph Hollibaugh.)

This photograph was taken after 1927 and shows the tracks used to move ore from the Afterthought Mine to the smelter in Ingot. During the operation of the mine by the California Zinc Company, ore from the bunkers on the right was carried on an aerial tramway using 140 two-ton buckets to the smelter at Bully Hill. (Courtesy of Shasta Historical Society.)

A crew poses while working inside the Afterthought smelter between 1901 and 1907. The smelter was not only subject to closures due to worldwide copper prices, but because of its isolated location, it was subject to closure for lack of supplies. During the winter of 1906–1907, the smelter could not be supplied with flux, as the dirt access roads became a quagmire for supply wagons. The costly difficulties attending the smelting process closed the smelter in 1907, but some employees remained for at least two years to work in an experimental plant that attempted to find alternative ore processing methods. (Courtesy of Shasta Historical Society.)

The Ingot Post Office, shown on this postcard, was established in May 1904 and was discontinued in August 1940, when operations were moved to Bella Vista. Prior to the Ingot Post Office being established, the Kendon Post Office had been established in July 1900 on the east side of Cow Creek just north of Ingot. That post office closed in December 1900 after being open for just over four months. (Courtesy of Ralph Hollibaugh.)

Ingot is pictured around 1922. The town was originally known as Silverton. It was a shipping point for oblong bars of blister copper that came from the nearby smelter. Blister copper is about 98.5 percent pure and takes its name from the broken surface created by escaping sulfur dioxide gas during the cooling process. (Courtesy of Shasta Historical Society.)

The Ward Hotel in Ingot, seen here, and the nearby Olsen Boarding House were home to many of the employees of the Afterthought smelter. (Courtesy of Shasta Historical Society.)

The Terry lumber flume, on the left, ran through Ingot as well as on the creek side of the smelter and Afterthought Mine. The 32-mile flume ran from Hatchet Mountain to Bella Vista with a vertical drop of 3,675 feet. The flume was extended by Joseph Enright in 1886 before being purchased by Joseph Terry in 1897. Terry operated the flume until 1919, and from 1920 to 1922, it was operated by the Red River Lumber Company. After 1922, the flume was idle. (Courtesy of Shasta Historical Society.)

Three

KENNETT-MAMMOTH SMELTER
WEST SHASTA COPPER-ZINC DISTRICT

The West Shasta Copper-Zinc District rests in the Klamath Mountains along the west bank of the Sacramento River, centered on three principal mines: Mammoth to the north, Balaklala in the center, and Iron Mountain to the south. The Mammoth Mine is in the area between Squaw Creek (different than the Squaw Creek of the East Shasta Copper-Zinc District) and Little Backbone Creek and was opened to gold mining by the 1850s. The area was generally known as Backbone until 1884, when the Central Pacific Railroad moved north from Redding and established a siding along the Sacramento River. The siding was used as an emergency brake testing station and named Kennet after Squire Kennet, a major stockholder in the California & Oregon Railroad (owned by the Central Pacific Company by 1884). In about 1885, Charles Butters started buying 6,000 acres around the siding and laid out a townsite. Butters, who opened Butters' Ore Milling Works in Kennett, was a visionary who foresaw the major expansion of the copper industry centered around Kennett. In 1886, the Kennett Post Office was established, adding a "T" to the name. By 1907, the Mammoth Copper Company built a smelter at Kennett, and by 1910, the town was the second-largest population center in Shasta County with a population of 3,000. Kennett was incorporated in 1911, but the major boom only lasted until 1919. The decrease in demand for copper at the end of World War I, a corresponding drop in copper prices, and an increase in legal claims closed the smelter in 1919. Ore production from the Mammoth Mine and others continued, and the smelter opened periodically, but by 1925, the smelter was dismantled. By 1930, Kennett returned to unincorporated status. With the beginning of the Shasta Dam Project in 1935, the end of Kennett was projected. In March 1942, the railroad used the rerouted line to O'Brien summit, bypassing Kennett as the waters of the new Lake Shasta approached the town. Today, the townsite is about a mile north of Shasta Dam, marked by nearby Slaughterhouse Island (named for the Endicott slaughterhouse and meat market that was in the saddle below the current island).

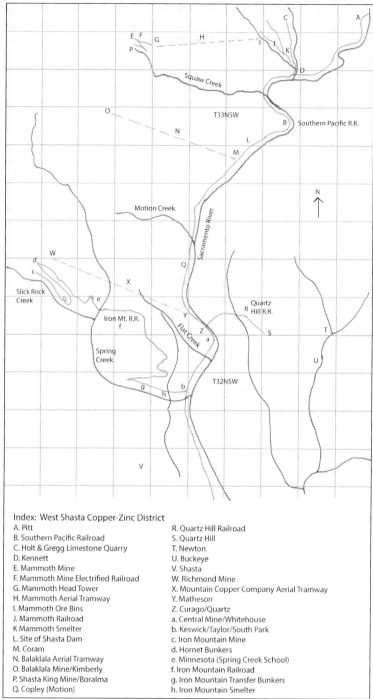

Index: West Shasta Copper-Zinc District

A. Pitt
B. Southern Pacific Railroad
C. Holt & Gregg Limestone Quarry
D. Kennett
E. Mammoth Mine
F. Mammoth Mine Electrified Railroad
G. Mammoth Head Tower
H. Mammoth Aerial Tramway
I. Mammoth Ore Bins
J. Mammoth Railroad
K Mammoth Smelter
L. Site of Shasta Dam
M. Coram
N. Balaklala Aerial Tramway
O. Balaklala Mine/Kimberly
P. Shasta King Mine/Boralma
Q. Copley (Motion)

R. Quartz Hill Railroad
S. Quartz Hill
T. Newton
U. Buckeye
V. Shasta
W. Richmond Mine
X. Mountain Copper Company Aerial Tramway
Y. Matheson
Z. Curago/Quartz
a. Central Mine/Whitehouse
b. Keswick/Taylor/South Park
c. Iron Mountain Mine
d. Hornet Bunkers
e. Minnesota (Spring Creek School)
f. Iron Mountain Railroad
g. Iron Mountain Transfer Bunkers
h. Iron Mountain Smelter

The West Shasta Copper-Zinc District benefited by access to the California & Oregon Railroad, which had begun to move north from Redding through the Sacramento River Canyon in 1882. The railroad line connected San Francisco and Portland in 1887. The C&ORR was a subsidiary of the Southern Pacific Railroad but continued to operate under its own name into the 1890s. (Courtesy of Andrew Jolliff.)

This photograph shows Southern Pacific Railroad cars as they enter Kennett. In 1884, the railroad established a spur at Kennet, but in 1886, the US Post Office took the name Kennett, and both seemed to be used interchangeably. (Courtesy of Shasta Historical Society.)

This view of Kennett from the east side of the Sacramento River shows the Southern Pacific rail line just above the east bank and the town stretched out up the hills. The Mammoth smelter is to the left, just outside of town. As the town grew, suburbs and shantytowns grew right up to the smelter property. (Courtesy of Shasta Historical Society.)

The railroad depot clearly shows that the railroad used the name Kennet rather than Kennett. The railroad printed its timetables, advertisements, and other material using this name. Nearby Redding was named by the California & Oregon Railroad for employee Benjamin Bernard Redding. In 1874, the legislature changed the name to Reading for local landowner Pierson B. Reading. The railroad continued to print its material as Redding, and in 1880 had the original name restored. Throughout the copper boom, the railroads held immense power in Shasta County through control of shipping costs and other logistics. (Courtesy of Shasta Historical Society.)

The first Golinsky Hotel in 1888, shown here, was established by Bernhard Golinsky. Seated on the bench in the foreground are, from left to right, Bernhard, his wife Rosa, his nieces Martha and Henrietta, and nephew Jake. Bernhard was often referred to as the "father of Kennett" and founded a 160-acre subdivision known as Bernhard. Jake managed the Kennet Hotel and the Golinsky Store in Keswick and was postmaster of Taylor. (Courtesy of Shasta Historical Society.)

The second Kennet Hotel and Bar shown here was locally known as the Golinsky Hotel. It was constructed across several lots on the site of the old Whitten Store, Rooming House, and Saloon that had opened in 1884. The new structure featured a bar and dining room with 100 sleeping rooms, each wired for electricity and sanitary plumbing. Bernhard Golinsky's hotel was the Kennet Hotel, but the address was in Kennett. In 1884, the siding was named for Squire Kennet, one of the stockholders who made the inspection trip when the railroad built through the Sacramento River Canyon from Redding toward Oregon. The post office was established in 1886 and took the name of the siding but spelled it with a double "T." In March 1942, the Southern Pacific Railroad opened the new route over O'Brien summit, and the post office closed, moving operations to Summit City. (Courtesy of Ralph Hollibaugh.)

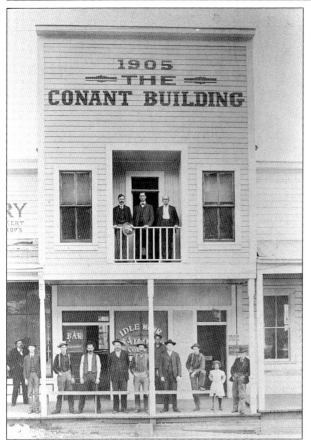

In 1920, the Trinity Copper Company, which operated the Shasta King, Lost Desert, and King Copper groups, went out of business and sold its properties to G.A. Haskell of Boston. Haskell immediately sold the property to the newly organized Trinity Copper Corporation of Virginia for $1. Stock certificates, such as the one shown here, were still being sold in 1924, but the corporation appears to have only leased the 1,200-acre property for short periods and was in financial trouble. (Courtesy of Ralph Hollibaugh.)

In December 1904, a fire started in the Smithson Saloon and destroyed the business district on the south side of the railroad tracks, including the offices of the Mammoth Copper Company. By 1905, most of the town was rebuilt, including the Conant Building, shown here, which was owned by Justice of the Peace J.N. Conant. (Courtesy of Shasta Historical Society.)

The new Kennett fire bell was installed in 1912 for Kennett Hose Company No. 1, which stored its hand-drawn equipment inside the structure. Kennett had suffered a devastating fire in 1904, and in response, much of the town was rebuilt using brick. (Courtesy of Shasta Historical Society.)

The Castle Rock Saloon and Butters' building in Kennett are shown in this photograph. Charles Butters was a mining engineer who had developed a method of processing ore by chlorination and surveyed land in Kennett in about 1888 for his plant, Butters' Ore Milling Works. In addition, Butters purchased several thousand acres around Kennett with the idea of building an ideal upper-class city. On the issue of town development, Butters was often at odds with "the Father of Kennett," Bernard Golinsky. The Castle Rock Saloon was just one of 40 operating during the copper boom. (Courtesy of Shasta Historical Society.)

This photograph shows the Kennett Hotel. Note that the hotel operated by the Golinsky family was the Kennet Hotel; the Kennett Hotel was a separate entity. (Courtesy of Shasta Historical Society.)

The Kern barbershop in Kennett is seen here, probably around 1905. Edwin Kern was born in 1880 and, like many merchants, moved with the whims of the economy. In 1900, he operated a barbershop in Redding, and by 1910 was operating a barbershop farther north in the Sacramento Canyon at Delta. (Courtesy of Shasta Historical Society.)

The Kennett School was organized in 1890 and eventually served a population of 10,000. In 1905, a bond issue allowed the construction of a new school, shown here, which in 1923 was still serving 116 students. (Courtesy of Shasta Historical Society.)

The reverse of this photograph lists these teachers in Kennett as, from left to right, Bertha Bass, Alice Dunham, Ethel Jackson Rose, Jennie Cooper, and Josie Mullen. The photograph was probably taken prior to 1910, as Bertha Bass, the daughter of local merchant Hebert Bass, was teaching in Round Mountain by 1910. Josie Mullen, the daughter of Redding livery stable owner James Mullen, was teaching in Redding by 1910. Most school districts preferred short contracts to tenured teachers, so it was common for teachers to work at five or more schools during their careers. (Courtesy of Shasta Historical Society.)

The Mammoth Copper Company built the hospital shown here for the employees of the mine and smelter, but it did accept other residents of Kennett. The hospital, which was built about 1908, could manage minor surgeries, but more serious cases had to be transferred to Redding. The company hospital closed in 1919. Note the outhouse at the left front corner of the building. When the hospital closed, a group of local doctors rented space in the Kennet Hotel as a replacement hospital for a number of years. (Courtesy of Shasta Historical Society.)

This photograph is of V.E. Warren's Diamond Saloon in Kennett. Victor Eugene "Slim" Warren had a passion for diamonds and was always seen wearing a diamond stickpin. Warren started the Diamond Saloon in 1904 on Railroad Avenue at the depot, only to have it burn down the same year. By 1906, he had opened a new brick structure that became the best-known business in Kennett. Warren added 40 rooms in 1907 and an upper floor to serve food. Eventually, the structure was four stories, with a bar, restaurant, and gambling area, and included a distillery and bottling room. At its peak, the Diamond Saloon operated 24 hours a day and employed 16 men on each of its three shifts. (Courtesy of Ralph Hollibaugh.)

This postcard shows the interior of the Diamond Café. The postcard may date from the Prohibition era, when Warren put his best stock of alcohol in a bonded warehouse and concentrated on meals for railroad passengers. V.E. Warren furnished the Diamond Saloon in a lavish manner, but he wisely invested his money. By the end of the copper boom, he had transitioned to lumber and land, especially at Hilt in Siskiyou County. (Courtesy of Ralph Hollibaugh.)

It was not noted if the Mammoth Band shown here was organized at the smelter or the Mammoth Mine. At its peak, the Mammoth Mine and smelter employed 2,300 workers from around the world. (Courtesy of Shasta Historical Society.)

The Methodist Episcopal church was built using material from the former church in Keswick. It was started in 1906; around the same time, Catholic and Baptist churches were also started. For a short period from 1906 to 1907, Rev. J.J. Pardee, a cousin to the governor of California, was a minister. (Courtesy of Shasta Historical Society.)

This photograph shows the Catholic church at Kennett. By 1906, the hills behind the church were almost devoid of vegetation from a combination of overcutting and the effects of sulfur dioxide fumes from the roasting and smelting process. (Courtesy of Shasta Historical Society.)

The Mammoth Copper Company was considered progressive as it provided multi-room married housing quarters, as shown here, for its smelter employees. Management housing was more substantial and contained all the luxury furnishings as those in the best parts of Redding, and management had a shorter work week and access to a wider range of leisure and social activities. Laborers at the smelter were still working 60 hours per week in 1910, but there was competition for employment, as the pay was above that of common laborers and the work was steady for long periods. (Courtesy of Shasta Historical Society.)

The photograph shows a swinging bridge across Backbone Creek leading to the Mammoth smelter. The bridge provided easier access for employees from Kennett. (Courtesy of Shasta Historical Society.)

This image shows the Mammoth smelter with the baghouse to the rear. The baghouse was installed after lawsuits and was intended to reduce copper sulfide and particle emissions by filtering the air. The baghouse complied with the intent of the court's orders and allowed the smelters to continue operations, but in the end, they could not meet the high filtration efficiency needed to protect crops, and lawsuits were renewed. The smokestack at center was 12 feet in diameter and 150 feet high. (Courtesy of Shasta Historical Society.)

The inside of the bullion room at the Mammoth smelter appears to have stacks of copper ingots ready for shipment. The ingots were between 98.5 and 99.5 percent pure copper and were transported over the Southern Pacific Railroad to other locations for the final refining process. (Courtesy of Shasta Historical Society.)

The Mammoth smelter is shown dumping slag. For every ton of copper produced, the smelter generated 2.2 tons of slag. The slag, which contained iron, alumina, calcium oxide, and silica, was dumped as ingots, diluted with water to form granules, or poured in molten form into the canyon at Backbone Creek, creating future environmental problems. (Courtesy of Shasta Historical Society.)

This photograph shows the dumping of cooled slag from the convertor at the smelter. Copper matte was produced by flash smelting and then transferred to a convertor furnace, where enriched oxygen is blown into the matte, creating blister copper that is 98.5 to 99.5 percent pure. (Courtesy of Shasta Historical Society.)

As technology improved, an electrolytic zinc plant, shown here, was installed at the Mammoth smelter. The plant produced the only reported recovery of cadmium in California from 1917 to 1918. The mineral, usually found associated with zinc, was valued as it was resistant to corrosion and used to plate steel. (Courtesy of Shasta Historical Society.)

The outskirts of Kennett became known as "Dago Town" and were created by an influx of Italian workers seeking steady employment at the Mammoth smelter. "Little Italy," as it was also known, was very much an example of the major two-class social system that developed in Kennett. Little Italy went on to develop its own stores, gambling houses, saloons, and banking system headed by Antonio Carattini. New immigrants could not afford houses in Butters's upper-class subdivision or the middle-class houses at Bernard. (Courtesy of Shasta Historical Society.)

Access to the east side of the Sacramento River was reached by the Kennett ferry. In January and February 1907, there was a devastating flood, and a ferry carrying immigrant Greek workers overturned, killing 11. (Courtesy of Shasta Historical Society.)

The Sacramento River bridge at Kennett replaced the ferry and greatly improved access from the east side of the river. The bridge was built about 1915 and had a sign on the east side stating, "walk your horses, autos slow to 10 MPH or pay $25.00 fine." (Courtesy of Shasta Historical Society.)

In this photograph of the Mammoth Mine, the row of buildings at center appear to hang almost over the edge. The buildings were, from left to right, the boardinghouse, tram terminal, compressor room, blacksmith shop, and the mine office. For the benefit of the employees living at the Mammoth Mine, a post office was opened in 1907 and took its name from the Mammoth Copper Mining Company. As operations at the mine slowed, the Mammoth Post Office was closed in 1921 but reopened between 1923 and 1925 when the mine was again active. Postal operations were moved to Kennett in 1925. (Courtesy of Ralph Hollibaugh.)

This image shows the street at the Mammoth Mine that appeared to be hanging onto the ridge face in the previous illustration. This view looks toward the mine office and shows the social hall to the left and the bunkhouse to the right. (Courtesy of Shasta Historical Society.)

Frank Johnson and Bob Roach are seen drilling at the Mammoth Mine. The ore bodies were up to 110 feet thick, with the uppermost portion having a higher zinc content. Between 1905 and 1925, a total of 3,311,145 tons of ore were removed from the mine, containing 3.99 percent copper, 4.20 percent zinc, 2.24 ounces of silver per ton, and 0.038 ounces of gold per ton. From 1914 to 1915, about 84,000 tons of ore were produced with zinc, accounting for 21.1 percent. (Courtesy of Shasta Historical Society.)

This photograph shows miners on break at an entrance to the Mammoth Mine. The mine had nine primary entrances, or adits, entering the mountain between the 2,426-foot and 3,096-foot elevations. (Courtesy of Shasta Historical Society.)

A miner is using a diamond drill to begin a new entrance (adit). Diamond drills were often used for exploration as the core drill bits could withdraw a small diameter core of rock to analyze. (Courtesy of Shasta Historical Society.)

A rescue team at the Mammoth Mine is shown in this photograph. Cave-ins and blasting accidents were a fact of life in the mines, but miners suffered equally from occupational diseases. After the introduction of the pneumatic hammer drill in 1897, there was an increase in the lung disease silicosis, commonly known as white lung, to differentiate it from its coal mine relative. The Mammoth mining operations were considered progressive in both training of rescue teams and providing medical care at the hospital in Kennett. (Courtesy of Shasta Historical Society.)

Miners are breaking an entrance at the 500-foot level. The level refers to the shaft level, not the elevation. The main haulage adit was at the 470-foot level, which corresponds to 2,820 feet above sea level. The ore train at the 470-foot level traveled five miles underground. (Courtesy of Shasta Historical Society.)

The head of the gravity road at Mammoth Mine is shown here. Ore was delivered by mine cars to the head tower and then sent down a two-mile gravity road for transportation to the smelter. (Courtesy of Shasta Historical Society.)

This is a view from the bottom of the gravity road at the Mammoth Mine. The buildings at the bottom were ore storage bins. (Courtesy of Shasta Historical Society.)

The aerial tramway at the Mammoth Mine is shown here. By 1907, the tramway was proving inadequate to handle the ore production and was replaced by the Mammoth Railroad. At the same time, a spur line was built at Central Mine that connected with the Southern Pacific Railroad, mainly to provide flux for the smelter. (Courtesy of Shasta Historical Society.)

This image shows copper precipitation tanks at the Mammoth Mine. The tanks were used to remove much of the commercially worthless material from the ore, thus reducing or concentrating the ore for shipment down to the smelter. The process reduced the load on the gravity road and tramway, but the resulting tailings were simply dumped outside the mine. (Courtesy of Shasta Historical Society.)

The Fourth of July celebration was a high point of the year for many workers. This group is walking to the baseball field on the ridge above the Mammoth Mine after other activities such as a picnic, foot races, mucking contests, and more were concluded at the mine. (Courtesy of Shasta Historical Society.)

The 1914 Fourth of July celebration at the Mammoth Mine began at 4:00 a.m. with a case of dynamite being set off at the mine dump. A picnic was held on Little Backbone Creek, and the day was filled with games and races that included rock-drilling, wrestling, and mucking contests for the miners. Egg races and other more refined activities were available for the more genteel set. (Courtesy of Shasta Historical Society.)

These miners are competing in a Fourth of July drilling contest. Much like rodeos that featured events that evolved from day-to-day activities of cowboys, miners developed their own events such as mucking and drilling. In the drilling contest, competitors were judged on which team could drill deepest in a set time, as if preparing for blasting. (Courtesy of Shasta Historical Society.)

Each year, there was a baseball tournament on the ridge at the Mammoth Mine, with multiple teams invited from across the county. This was the highlight of every Fourth of July celebration at the Mammoth Mine. (Courtesy of Shasta Historical Society.)

The Holt and Gregg Limestone Quarry near Kennett was located on Little Backbone Creek at about the 2,000-foot level, and the limestone initially was roasted in a kiln to produce cement as early as 1884. In about 1900, three new kilns using crude oil were built on the edge of Kennett. The limestone was moved by electric railroad, with power supplied by the Northern California Power Company. Broken limestone from the quarry was also used as flux at the smelter. The Kennett limestone works closed in 1920. (Courtesy of Shasta Historical Society.)

This photograph shows ore bins at the Holt & Gregg limestone quarry. James Holt was a brick maker, and John Gregg a brick mason. Holt operated the company's brick plants at Redding and Anderson while Gregg managed the lime works at Kennett. The initial purpose of the quarry was to produce cement, but the demand for flux at the smelter altered its usage. (Courtesy of Shasta Historical Society.)

This image shows the kiln at the Holt & Gregg quarry. In 1905, the Balaklala Consolidated Copper Company alone placed an order for one million bricks for its smelter at Coram. (Courtesy of Shasta Historical Society.)

Four

Coram-Balaklala Mine
West Shasta Copper-Zinc District

The history of Coram stems directly from the development of the Balaklala Mine. The mine took its name from native Wintu for "windy place" and was first worked in the 1890s. In 1902, the mine was purchased by eastern financiers, including Guggenheim, for its copper potential. By 1905, the Balaklala Consolidated Mining Company decided to establish a smelter near the Sacramento River, and shortly afterward began selling town lots. An aerial tramway was constructed from the mine to carry ore to the smelter, and the short Balaklala Railroad was constructed to connect the smelter to the Southern Pacific siding opened in January 1907. Two distinct communities developed: Coram around the smelter and Kimberly at the mine site on West Squaw Creek, both connected by a steep, five-mile dirt road.

Coram quickly blossomed into a town with between 1,000 and 2,000 residents, a telephone system, an electrical system, and 23 saloons. The town quickly filed for incorporation, and the school district, jail, and stores served surrounding mining communities, such as the Shasta King Mine. The boom ended in 1911 when an injunction closed the smelter due to damage from sulfur dioxide fumes that had destroyed crops and fruit orchards as far away as Cottonwood. The company struggled with a means of controlling the emission problems until 1914, before closing the smelter permanently. The Balaklala Mine continued to produce copper, shipping it first to Kennett, then as far as Tacoma, Washington. In 1918, the remaining citizens of Coram voted for disincorporation, and the town quickly declined. By 1928, the Balaklala Mine had ceased production, and Coram all but disappeared, except for a short reprieve during the construction of Shasta Dam.

here is where you get off the town is one mile from here the red cross is the depot but we'll have a new one this summer the stream is the Sacramento the Red X is the Depot. The other buildings are Saloons

This postcard shows the Coram depot in 1906. The notations state that the other buildings closer to the Sacramento River were saloons. With the establishment of the Balaklala smelter, the site bloomed almost overnight. Shortly after the establishment of the town of Coram in 1906, a post office was opened and named for Joseph Arthur Coram, a mining financier who had started companies in Montana and Mexico as well as the Balaklala Consolidated Copper Company. When the smelter closed in 1911, the town was greatly depopulated, but the mine continued to operate, and there was enough business to keep the post office open until 1922, when operations were moved to Kennett. (Courtesy of Ralph Hollibaugh.)

This postcard shows Coram in 1907. The initial town was built on lots sold by the Balaklala Consolidated Copper Company, but within the year, others were selling lots in "East Coram." (Courtesy of Ralph Hollibaugh.)

This photograph shows Main Street in Coram in 1907. At best, the main roads were macadamized with compacted layers of broken stone, but most remained dirt and were subject to becoming quagmires in the winter when wagons churned the mud. (Courtesy of Ralph Hollibaugh.)

Coram, as shown in this 1909 photograph, had continued to grow as entrepreneurs purchased more land outside of the lots sold by the Bakalala Consolidated Copper Company. Flat land was at a premium, as this photograph demonstrates, forcing some businesses like the small building on the right to be built precariously close to the cliff edges. (Courtesy of Ralph Hollibaugh.)

This image shows the L.R. Rogers store in Coram. Rogers also operated a store at the Balaklala Mine, in which the Kimberly Post Office was located. (Courtesy of Ralph Hollibaugh.)

The Ames Hotel in Coram is shown here. John Wesley Ames was typical of many merchants living with the fluctuations of the copper economy, as he started in Redding, then was a caterer and hotel operator in Coram, and later worked in Ingot. (Courtesy of Ralph Hollibaugh.)

Shortly after Coram was established, 10 saloons were authorized by the county supervisors. The number grew to 23, many with gambling halls in the rear. Reportedly not one cent was collected from taxes to support the city, as the income from those 23 saloons paid the towns' expenses. Coram was also noted for having no churches. (Courtesy of Ralph Hollibaugh.)

This photograph shows the Southern Pacific Railroad tracks entering Coram. The large building on the hill is the Coram School. The school district began in 1907 after the Balaklala Consolidated Copper Company built a temporary school to serve 120 children. In 1908, the four-room school, modeled on the school at Kennett, was built. The school district lapsed in 1921. (Courtesy of Ralph Hollibaugh.)

This postcard shows a view from Main Street of Coram on the right, with the railroad tracks just above. The view looks toward the smelter. (Courtesy of Ralph Hollibaugh.)

This image shows the McCormick, Saeltzer & Company store at Coram. McCormick, Saeltzer & Company was based in Redding and was commonly called the "Big Store." The company opened subsidiary stores in many of the mining towns, such as Delamar and Keswick, and developed its own delivery system to support the outlying stores. The company operated its own feed and stock ranch at Clear Creek, just south of Redding. (Courtesy of Shasta Historical Society.)

This is a view inside the McCormick, Saeltzer & Company store at Coram. The store developed along modern departmental lines from farm equipment, hardware, and clothing to groceries and would deliver from its large store in Redding to subsidiary stores. (Courtesy of Shasta Historical Society.)

This is the bricklayer's baseball team at Coram in 1906. In 1905, the Bakalala Consolidated Copper Company made an initial purchase of one million bricks, and the bricklaying crew was responsible for building the smelter foundation and chimney. The crew worked at Coram until 1908, when the smelter was "blown in," or placed in operation. (Courtesy of Ralph Hollibaugh.)

The water tower at Coram is seen here along with a Southern Pacific crane that was commonly dispatched to repair tracks or bridges. When the tracks were pushed north from Redding in 1882, water stops were created every seven to ten miles to service the steam trains. Larger depots also provided wood or, later, coal. As the steam trains were converted to diesel oil, many of the water stops were closed. (Courtesy of Shasta Historical Society.)

The Balaklala smelter at Coram was built in 1906 and touted as the "million-dollar smelter" and the largest and most modern on the Pacific Coast, but was in operation only until 1911. The smelter could process 1,000 tons of ore per day, but the resulting sulfur dioxide caused damage to surrounding forest and agricultural land. The smelter was closed temporarily by court order in 1911 and permanently in 1914 after no solution could be found to the pollution problem. It was dismantled in 1920, and much of the ironworks moved to Bully Hill. (Courtesy of Ralph Hollibaugh.)

The smokestack at the Balaklala smelter was an impressive 275 feet tall, but began to crack after 18 months of operation. Some cite the crack as being caused by excessive heat and others a lightning strike. The smokestack was dynamited in 1913, and Holt & Gregg were contracted to build a shorter 250-foot stack. The new smokestack was a feature at Coram until 1926, when it too was dynamited. (Courtesy of Ralph Hollibaugh.)

The railroad siding at the Balaklala smelter in Coram is seen here after 1913. Stock documents list the Balaklala Copper Company as operating a private railroad and having five locomotives, presumably switcher engines, for use in the smelter siding. (Courtesy of Ralph Hollibaugh.)

The three-step processing of copper ore consisted of roasting, smelting, and converting. In the smelting stage, bulk impurities were removed to create a matte that was roughly 45 percent pure copper. The matte was then processed in a convertor furnace to again reduce the impurities. The convertor furnace introduced compressed oxygen from a compressor plant, as shown here at the Balaklala smelter, and the result was the production of blister copper that was 98.5 to 99.5 percent pure copper. (Courtesy of Ralph Hollibaugh.)

This photograph was taken inside the smelter as blister copper ingots are being poured. Note that the ingots are being moved by an electric car that is clearly labeled Balaklala Consolidated Copper Company, so it dates after 1905. (Courtesy of Ralph Hollibaugh.)

Slag is being dumped after being hauled from the smelter by electric car. The slag appears to have been mixed with water, which creates the granules seen on the ground. Slag is the byproduct left over after copper has been separated from the raw ore. In the Shasta Copper-Zinc Districts, iron formed a high percentage of the discarded slag. (Courtesy of Ralph Hollibaugh.)

The Balaklala Mine is seen here in winter. The mine site was named Kimberly after Peter J. Kimberley, the president of the Balaklala Mining Company of San Francisco. That company was taken over by the First National Copper Company in 1905, which operated under the Balaklala Consolidated Copper Company name. (Courtesy of Ralph Hollibaugh.)

The Balaklala Mine was initially worked in 1890, but its prime production period was from 1906 to 1911, when operations ceased. The mine was working again between 1914 to 1919 and then leased from 1924 to 1928. After the Balaklala smelter closed, ore was shipped first to the Mammoth smelter and then as far as Washington. (Courtesy of Ralph Hollibaugh.)

This photograph is labeled "Glory Hole" at the Balaklala Mine in 1909. The term has several meanings depending on the type of method used to extract the ore. Here, it is used to mean a deep-mine shaft. The Balaklala Mine had about 20 adits, with the main haulage tunnel being 1,500 feet long and serving 4,500 feet of drifts. (Courtesy of Ralph Hollibaugh.)

Employees and family members are seen at the branch office of the Rogers Store at the Balaklala Mine. The store also contained the Kimberly Post Office, which opened in 1907. Named after Peter J. Kimberly, the president of the Balaklala Mining Company of San Francisco, it remained open until December 1913, when operations were moved to Kennett. The mine was closed in 1914 but reopened from 1915 to 1919. The post office did not reopen. (Courtesy of Ralph Hollibaugh.)

Electric ore carts at the Balaklala Mine were used to deliver ore from the mine to the head tower for shipment to the smelter. They could efficiently carry supplies and miners as well as remove waste rock and ore, but initially were available only to larger mines with electrical power plants. With the development of the Keswick Electrical Company in 1901, the Mountain Copper Company secured electricity of a standard voltage. Keswick Electrical merged with the Redding Electric Company in 1902 to form the Northern California Power Company. By 1911, it was providing power throughout the East and West Shasta Copper-Zinc Districts. (Courtesy of Ralph Hollibaugh.)

The Balaklala Mine head tower is where ore from the mine was loaded on the aerial tramway for shipment to the smelter in Coram. The head tower also served the Shasta King and other mines in the area. The tramway was 16,500 feet long. (Courtesy of Ralph Hollibaugh.)

This image shows the loading buckets at the upper terminal of the tram. The buckets would carry up to 1,000 tons of ore per day. (Courtesy of Ralph Hollibaugh.)

This photograph shows the headworks of Shasta King Mine. The main adit was at the 1,816-foot elevation and extended 800 feet into the mountain. Many of the production values were not listed, but during the 1918–1919 lease, 68,889 tons of ore were produced, with 2.92 percent being copper, 1.01 ounce per ton of silver, and 0.034 ounce per ton of gold. What was uncommon was that zinc was zero percent. (Courtesy of Ralph Hollibaugh.)

Shasta King Mine was also where the Boralma Post Office was established in 1901. Both histories were entwined with the Trinity Copper Company, which operated the Shasta King Mine (Lost Desert, Trinity) at the site from 1902 to 1909. The origin of the name *Boralma* is unknown, but it is a surname, and the site may have been named for an earlier gold miner, or it may stem from the famous racehorse Boralma, who was active in the period from 1899 to 1902. The mine had about 15,000 feet of underground workings, and the ore was sent down a 2,000-foot incline tram before being transported to the head tower of the Balaklala tram for shipment to the Balaklala smelter at Coram. By 1906, the post office was closed, and operations moved to Kennett. The mine was totally idle from 1909 to 1917. The United States Smelting, Refining, and Mining Company later leased the mine in 1918 and operated it until 1919, shipping the ore to its smelter at Kennett. In 1919, the mine camp was totally destroyed by fire. (Courtesy of Ralph Hollibaugh.)

By 1907, the holdings of the Balaklala Copper Company were practically bankrupt, and its 10 percent bonds, shown here, were almost unsalable. The company was reorganized as the First National Copper Company through a complicated process. The First National Copper Company took over the Balaklala stock issue, and 98 percent of stockholders transferred stock to the new company. The smelter closed in 1911, but the mine continued to operate until 1928. (Courtesy of Ralph Hollibaugh.)

This image shows the "lordships" (British management) playing polo in Shasta. In 1896, the Mountain Copper Company brought over a group of 40 English bachelors, including the earl of Renwick, to work the administrative offices. This group and other English employees formed their own colony with cricket matches and all things English. (Courtesy of Ralph Hollibaugh.)

Five

KESWICK–IRON MOUNTAIN MINE

WEST SHASTA COPPER-ZINC DISTRICT

The southernmost section of the West Shasta Copper-Zinc District, lying nearest to Redding and near the old county seat of Shasta, had a long mining history. The area around Keswick was known as Hogtown by 1849 and later as Stump Ranch when mined for placer gold. Nearby Iron Mountain was noted by 1860 for iron deposits that were not developed, but this changed in 1879 when James Sallee found the exposed ore to be rich in silver. Sallee, with partners William Magee and Charles Camden, operated or leased the Iron Mountain Mine to recover silver and gold, but when complex sulfide ore, high in copper, was reached, production decreased. In the early 1890s, Iron Mountain's copper potential was brought to the attention of Matheson & Company of London, which had been operating the huge Rio Tinto Copper Mine in Spain. Matheson & Company organized Mountain Mines Ltd. in 1894 to purchase the Iron Mountain Mine, and in 1896 transferred the interests to Mountain Copper Company for development. Mountain Copper Company began work on a smelter on Spring Creek about a mile from the Southern Pacific siding established at Keswick in January 1896. At the same time, Mountain Copper Company began building the Iron Mountain Railroad to connect the mine, smelter, and railroad depot at Keswick.

The town of Keswick quickly grew to a population of over 1,000 in support of the smelter, while the separate community at the Iron Mountain Mine took the name of Fielding. The Mountain Copper Company smelter was closed in 1907 by court order, but production at the mine continued. In response to the smelter closure, Mountain Copper Company constructed a new smelter at Martinez in Contra Costa County. At the close of World War I, copper prices fell drastically, causing the Mountain Copper Company to adapt. In 1920, an aerial tramway was constructed from the Company's Richmond-Hornet group to a receiving plant at Matheson, farther north on the Sacramento River. Mountain Copper Company focused on new uses for the ore in fertilizers and munitions. In 1923, Mountain Copper moved its headquarters to Matheson. Keswick slowly closed, and the Iron Mountain Railroad ceased carrier status in 1927, although housing at the Old Mine continued to be used during operations at the Richmond-Hornet Mine and the open pit operations at Brick Flat. In 1969, the operation of the aerial tramway to Matheson closed, spelling the end of Mountain Copper Company's operations in Shasta County. In the 1960s, Keswick had a reprieve as a bedroom community of Redding, only to be devastated in the Carr fire of 2018.

The Keswick Hotel and the McCormick, Saeltzer & Company store brought the best of Redding to the development of Keswick. In 1899, H.H. Noble contracted with Lord Keswick to form the Keswick Electric Company to supply electric power to the smelter at Keswick. By 1901, Keswick Electric was supplying electric power to Redding and north to the town of Keswick from the company's new power plant at Volta on Battle Creek. In 1902, Keswick Electric consolidated to form the Northern California Power Company, which supplied electric power to most of the copper mining towns. In 1919, Northern California Power Company merged to become Pacific Gas & Electric Company. (Courtesy of Ralph Hollibaugh.)

This photograph of the bridge at Keswick shows that it ran perpendicular to the Southern Pacific Railroad's tracks. Eight days after the railroad established a depot at Keswick, the post office followed suit. The townsite was named for Lord William Keswick, the president of Mountain Copper Company, and the post office kept the name. In 1923, when the Mountain Copper Company transferred its headquarters to Matheson, the post office closed. (Courtesy of Ralph Hollibaugh.)

Louis Samuel Schuckman, shown here second from left, was the postmaster of Keswick from November 1897 to October 1899. This photograph was taken at the Keswick depot, where he was employed as a railroad agent. Schuckman was noted for stopping a robbery by shooting one of the masked robbers. His wife, Ida, is at far left. (Courtesy of Ralph Hollibaugh.)

This photograph shows the Riverside Hotel next to the Keswick depot. The hotel may have been associated with the Southern Pacific Railroad, as Louis Samuel Schuckman managed both the hotel and railroad depot. In 1900, Schuckman and his wife, Ida, were admitted to the San Gabriel Sanatorium. Both died of tuberculosis in 1904. (Courtesy of Ralph Hollibaugh.)

In 1896, the Mountain Copper Company built its smelter, naming the site Keswick after chairman Lord William Keswick. The town quickly grew to a population of over 1,000 residents and had all the infrastructure of nearby Redding, including schools, a volunteer fire department, and stores, such as the one shown here in 1898. Prior to establishing the town, the area was sparsely populated and known as Stump Ranch for owner T.J. Stump. (Courtesy of Ralph Hollibaugh.)

The Methodist Episcopal church at Keswick, built in 1901 (moved to Kennett in 1906), is shown here. The hills behind the church were almost devoid of vegetation from the effects of the sulfur dioxide released from the smelter. (Courtesy of Shasta Historical Society.)

This image shows the area known as South Park, with Paradise Ally in the foreground. In 1896, Bernhard Golinsky of Kennett built a branch store and hotel at South Park, a suburb of Keswick that had grown up around the smelter. Bernhard's nephew Jake Golinsky was brought in to manage the operation. In 1897, the Taylor Post Office was opened at the Golinsky Store. Keswick had grown to be the second-largest town in Shasta County, and in 1897 had three post offices: Keswick, Taylor, and a small railroad post office at the depot. The railroad post office was closed in 1899, and operations were moved to Taylor. The post office was named in honor of Clay W. Taylor, who had been an attorney for the Mountain Copper Company, Shasta County district attorney from 1870 to 1882, and state senator from 1883 to 1886. As the copper boom declined, the smelter closed, and the Taylor Post Office was closed in 1922 when operations were moved to Kennett. In addition to Keswick having three post offices, at its peak, it had 35 saloons. (Courtesy of Ralph Hollibaugh.)

The notation on this photograph states that it shows the Keswick baseball team, but that the individual on the left in the second row is Robert "Bob" Hiatt from the Quartz Hill team. The Keswick team included Skinny Collins, George Eckles, Joe Jones, Mickey Cusick, Al Eleman, A.L. Jones, Charles Johnson, and Louie Fosta. (Courtesy of Shasta Historical Society.)

Many of the members of the Keswick Independent Band were drawn from the large immigrant population, especially Italians, Greeks, and Portuguese, who flocked to the mines and smelters looking for steady, good-paying employment. All the larger towns and mines generally had bands that played at employee dances or other special occasions, such as the Fourth of July, when the bands joined another universal entertainment: baseball. (Courtesy of Ralph Hollibaugh.)

Keswick School is shown here in 1898. Nellie Braynard, in the rear, was the teacher. Braynard was one of two teachers hired when the Campton School District was formed in 1897 and taught at least until 1903. The two-story school shown here was sold in 1923 by the Campton School District, which had moved to Matheson. (Courtesy of Ralph Hollibaugh.)

The smelter shown here was built in 1896 but was closed by 1904 by a lawsuit. A 1905 *San Francisco Call* article indicated that the Mountain Copper Company intended to run one of the four furnaces at the smelter and hire 300 men (reduced from 1,200 before the closure). At the same time, the company was to begin construction of a new smelter at Martinez in Contra Costa County. The smelter fully closed in 1907. The Iron Mountain Railroad can be seen in the background. (Courtesy of Ralph Hollibaugh.)

The Mountain Copper Company smelter was situated on Spring Creek. This photograph shows wastewater from the smelter being pumped directly into the creek. The houses on the hillside above the smelter were for management staff. (Courtesy of Ralph Hollibaugh.)

This image shows ore roasting for the Mountain Copper Company smelter. The demand for wood in the roasting process denuded the surrounding hills and added to the masses of copper sulfide fumes that killed crops and orchards in the Sacramento Valley to the south. The roasting process oxidized the ore before it was introduced into a reverberatory furnace. (Courtesy of Ralph Hollibaugh.)

Both the Mammoth Mine and the Iron Mountain Mine, shown here, had quarry crews to produce limestone flux for their smelters. The copper ore from the mine was transported to the smelter, where it was combined with local limestone flux to promote fluidity and remove impurities. It was the ready access to large deposits of limestone and quartz for use as flux that promoted the establishment of the copper and iron smelters. (Courtesy of Ralph Hollibaugh.)

The Iron Mountain Railroad needed to climb 1,850 feet in just 10.65 miles to connect the mine with the smelter near Keswick. The project was done from 1895 to 1896 and needed not only the 365-degree loop shown here, but two partial loops, a tunnel, and 25 trestles to create the proper grade. In 1915, the "Minnesota" mill was built midway along the railroad line and became California's first mill to use flotation concentration. The mill was closed in 1919. (Courtesy of Ralph Hollibaugh.)

The Iron Mountain Railroad is seen entering the 163-foot-long tunnel after crossing the principal trestle at Spring Creek. The Iron Mountain Railroad was incorporated in 1895, and was built under the supervision of Michael O'Shaughnessy, who went on to build San Francisco's Hetch Hetchy water project. (Courtesy of Ralph Hollibaugh.)

This Iron Mountain train is hauling wood to power the Mountain Copper Company smelter. The timber was picked up by boom on the Sacramento River after being floated down the Pit River. Prior to the Keswick Electrical Power Company supplying electrical power in 1901, the smelter had a 75-man lumber crew harvesting trees between Keswick and Copley, as well as contracting for wood from the Big Bend area of Shasta County. The train crew is listed as Ed Tucker, John Mirrow, Charles Shone, Dave Wells, and Thomas Sullivan. (Courtesy of Ralph Hollibaugh.)

This photograph shows the construction of a trestle on the Iron Mountain Railroad in 1895 or 1896. The railroad required 25 trestles, with the longest being 255 feet over Spring Creek. (Courtesy of Ralph Hollibaugh.)

This photograph shows "goats" on the Iron Mountain Railroad, which is a term for smaller locomotives designed for the hard work of assembling trains for long-distance hauling by larger engines. The term was extended to the workers who ran these engines with high starting tractive effort for getting heavy cars rolling. The goats, or switcher engines, were popular on short-distance railroads. The railroad started service with five wood-burning Porter engines. In 1901, the engines were converted to burn oil. The rolling stock, in addition to the engines, included 72 ore cars, 22 flat cars, and 2 cabooses. Permission was granted to abandon the railroad in 1927, and most of the rolling stock was moved to Matheson and scrapped. (Courtesy of Ralph Hollibaugh.)

The ready access to timber was an essential part of the operation of the larger mines. Here, the timber crew responsible for shoring and timbering thousands of feet of tunnels and shafts in the Iron Mountain Mine is coming off shift. Other timber crews harvested wood for the roasting process to prepare ore for the smelter. In this photograph, timber remains on the ridge, but within a short period, the huge demand for wood forced crews to find sources farther and farther from the mine and smelter. (Courtesy of Ralph Hollibaugh.)

In 1896, the Iron Mountain Mine was transferred to the Mountain Copper Company, and extensive development began. This photograph, titled "Iron Mountain as it used to be," probably dates from this period, when the focus of production changed from silver and gold to copper. In 1897, a fire destroyed the silver-processing building and many of the other mine structures, but all were quickly replaced and utilized until 1922. After 1922, the operations buildings began a slow process of decay and damage from erosion. The cottages were later utilized when the mine was opened again from 1931 to World War II to work the upper exposed ore deposits for gold. Mining also shifted to the Richmond and Hornet mines to produce pyrite ores. All underground mining ceased in 1956, and all mining operations ceased in 1963. (Courtesy of Ralph Hollibaugh.)

The 1897 Iron Mountain Mine fire destroyed the older processing area dedicated to the recovery of silver and gold, but within months, new structures covered the area. With most of the mine buildings constructed of wood and so many open heat sources, fire was a fact of life at the mines, just as it was in the mining towns. (Courtesy of Ralph Hollibaugh.)

The upper ore bunkers and end of the Iron Mountain Railroad are shown here. The ore was taken to the smelter on Spring Creek for the smelting and converting process before the blister copper ingots were transported to the depot at Keswick and transferred to the Southern Pacific Railroad for delivery. (Courtesy of Ralph Hollibaugh.)

The Iron Mountain Mine is a collection of nine underground mines and an open-pit mine that worked the gossan outcrop. This photograph is believed to show miners coming off shift at the Old Mine in the 1890s, as they are all carrying candles rather than carbide lamps that became popular after 1900. Behind the miners to the left is an adit, or horizontal entrance, to a tunnel driven thousands of feet into the mountain to reach the main ore body. (Courtesy of Ralph Hollibaugh.)

This photograph shows the boardinghouse (right) and off-duty miners at the Iron Mountain Mine sometime between 1896 and 1898. At the height of the copper boom in about 1906, there were two boardinghouses of 16 rooms each and staff quarters of 16 rooms. In addition, the company built 25 married cottages and four cottages for the manager and superintendents. (Courtesy of Ralph Hollibaugh.)

The Iron Mountain Mine is seen here in winter. From 1885 to 1886, the site was the location of the Iron Mountain Post Office, while the mine was leased for silver production. The Mountain Copper Company took over operations in 1896 and, for the benefit of its employees, provided space at its mine headquarters in the Mountain House Hotel for a new post office. The post office was named for Charles W. Fielding, who was on the board of the Mountain Copper Company and Iron Mountain Railway Company. The post office closed in 1903 when operations were moved to Taylor near the Mountain Copper Company smelter. (Courtesy of Ralph Hollibaugh.)

Due to the long shifts, an extended working week, and long distances to the Iron Mountain Mine, the Mountain Copper Company provided onsite services for its employees. In addition to bunkhouses and family cottages, the company built a large mess hall operated by cooks, such as those pictured here about 1897. The company also provided an entertainment hall for the employees that contained a kitchen and dining room as well as a canteen, billiard room, and music room. (Courtesy of Ralph Hollibaugh.)

Although desolate today, in the 1890s, James Spellman built a resort near the mine, the Mountain House Hotel, that became popular with local businessmen. In 1894, the hotel became headquarters of Mountain Mines Ltd., which became the Mountain Copper Company in 1896. The British management team encouraged good relations with the business and professional community; the team often entertained visitors and allowed some to use its 4,400 acres for recreational purposes. The visitors shown in this photograph stand in front of the mine superintendent's office and carry carbide lamps while the miners still utilize candles. (Courtesy of Ralph Hollibaugh.)

The overhead line type of electric engine went into use in Appalachian coal mines in 1887, and by 1903 was common in most large mines. The engines were used to move ore out of the mine and above ground to take the ore, often over extended distances, to storage bunkers for eventual transport to the smelter. (Courtesy of Ralph Hollibaugh.)

These three Mammoth Mine miners appear to be surveying the effects of blasting. Some of the orebodies, especially at the Old Mine, contained 7.5 percent copper, 1.00 ounce of silver per ton, and 0.04 ounces of gold per ton. The copper percentage for many currently operating copper mines is as low as 0.6 percent, and 2 percent is still considered high-grade ore. (Courtesy of Shasta Historical Society.)

The end of the copper boom decreased the productive value of the Iron Mountain Mine, but the Mountain Copper Company transferred its focus to the pyrite-rich ores of the nearby Hornet group, shown here, which included the Richmond Mine. Pyrite, or iron sulfide, was used for fertilizers, munitions, and refining petroleum and kept the mine operating until 1963. The crushing plant at the Richmond adit processed the ore for transportation on the aerial tram to the new company operation center at Matheson. The Matheson Post Office was established in 1922 and reportedly named for James Matheson, the founder of Matheson & Company, the parent company of Mountain Mines Company Ltd. of London. The manager of the company, when it purchased the Iron Mountain Mine in 1894, was Hugh Matheson, James's nephew, so it seems more likely to be named for him. In 1954, Matheson became a rural station of Redding and was finally closed in 1962. The Southern Pacific spur at Matheson was in operation until 1951, when the line was relocated due to construction of the Keswick Dam and renamed Kett for William F. Kett, general manager of the Mountain Copper Company. (Courtesy of Ralph Hollibaugh.)

In 1929, the Mountain Copper Company installed a cyanidation plant to start working on the gossan mine by the open-pit method, as seen here. Gossan is oxidized, weathered ore usually in the upper, exposed portion of a mine. The gossan is high in iron content, giving the mining scar seen today from Redding and Lake Shasta its rust color. In the 13 years after 1929, about 2.6 million tons of gossan were mined. (Courtesy of Ralph Hollibaugh.)

The cyanide tanks seen here were used for the leaching of gold and silver from copper ores. The use of cyanide was safer and more efficient than previous methods using mercury. The ore was crushed and put through a gravity separation before being placed in the cyanide tanks, where the gold was dissolved and separated. (Courtesy of Ralph Hollibaugh.)

This image shows the open-pit quarry mined for gold-bearing gossan lying over the old Iron Mountain Mine orebody. The gossans were a focus in 1879 and became of interest again with the installation of cyanide tanks to leach out gold. The vat-leaching method is more controlled than heap leaching, but the resulting waste known as tailings had to be stored behind large dams. Over time, drainage from the mine and tailings created the need to build the Spring Creek Debris Dam in 1963. The mine remains an Environmental Protection Agency Superfund site. (Courtesy of Shasta Historical Society.)

The employee residences at Iron Mountain Mine were built by the Mountain Copper Company around the turn of the 20th century for easy access of married miners to the mines. When operations moved to the Richmond and Hornet groups farther north along the ridge, the administrative and ore-processing buildings were deserted, but due to limited access, the married houses were reused, especially for the open-pit operations. (Courtesy of Ralph Hollibaugh.)

An aerial tram is being used by employees around 1940. Due to the steep terrain and limited road access, the tram was used to deliver household supplies to families living along the ridge. (Courtesy of Ralph Hollibaugh.)

A family is pictured at one of the employee residences at the Iron Mountain Mine. The residences were maintained, but the operations buildings were left to decay and were subject to being damaged from the effects of erosion. (Courtesy of Ralph Hollibaugh.)

The beginning of the road to the Iron Mountain Mine is seen here. The road runs under an ore chute at a loading bin along the Southern Pacific Railroad tracks. (Courtesy of Ralph Hollibaugh.)

This photograph shows the Iron Mountain School in 1932. The school was on Iron Mountain Road in an area known as Minnesota for the old Minnesota Mine. Keswick and the surrounding area were initially served by the Campton School District (named after an early gold miner). In 1955, the district combined with the Flat Creek School District to form the Spring Creek Union School District. (Courtesy of Ralph Hollibaugh.)

The Copley depot was established in 1884 between Keswick to the south and Coram to the north to serve the existing small town of Copley. Copley served as the main outlet for the gold mines of the Flat Creek Mining District that stretched along the Sacramento River from Spring Creek to Motion Creek. In 1886, a post office was established and took the name "Copley," but there is no definitive answer as to Copley's identity or if it was named for the local geologic feature, Copley greenstone, which was prominent at mines like the Diamond King. In 1891, the Southern Pacific changed the name of the depot to Motion, as shown here, while the post office continued with the Copley name until operations were moved to Kennett in 1913. (Courtesy of Shasta Historical Society.)

On the night of March 31, 1904, George and Vernon Gates, along with Shorty Arnett, entered the Southern Pacific express car as the train stopped at Copley to water the engines. The town was described as a water-tank town of two or three rows of scattered houses, a general store, a saloon, and the Southern Pacific water tank. After a gunfight that left a Wells, Fargo, and Company messenger dead, the robbers placed 20 sticks of dynamite on the top of the safe. The resulting explosion, shown in this photograph, destroyed the roof and side of the railcar and left enough debris in the safe that the robbers failed to find gold sacks lining the safe floor. The three robbers were quickly identified as George and Vernon Gates and Shorty Arnett, using a laundry mark found at the robbery site. George and Vernon were killed resisting arrest for another robbery in 1905 in New Mexico. Shorty Arnett was never apprehended. (Courtesy of Shasta Historical Society.)

Six

Quartz Hill–Buckeye
West Shasta Copper-Zinc District

The area known as Buckeye on the east side of the Sacramento River, just north of current Redding, was a center for placer mining as early as 1849. Portions of Buckeye were variously known as Grey Rocks, Old Diggings, and Quartz Hill, with considerable overlap over the years. Multiple small mining communities, such as Hart City, Quartz Hill City, and Bayha, sprang up around specific mines. Despite the confusion, the area had a common mining progression. Placer deposits were quickly worked out, and mining transitioned into quartz or lode mining after 1858, when gold was discovered in quartz veins, especially at Quartz Hill. By the end of the Civil War, the boom had subsided. After the California & Oregon Railroad (a subsidiary of the Central Pacific Railroad, reorganized as the Southern Pacific Railroad in 1885) pushed north from Redding in 1882 toward Delta, interest in the old dormant mines was rekindled. By 1892, the Calumet Mine had a tramway to the Southern Pacific line on the Sacramento River (closed in 1899). A little farther north, the Central Mine operated a tramway to Central Mine spur in 1890, and the Quartz Hill Mine hauled ore to the Quartz siding in 1897 (the name was changed to Cuargo in 1908). With the establishment of local smelters, many of the mines transitioned to sending low-grade copper ore for processing, but the event that connected the area to the West Shasta Copper-Zinc District came early around 1900, when the smelters needed flux to process copper ore. Gold and silver remained a byproduct of the mines, but by 1905, Mammoth Copper was leasing the Quartz Hill property for flux production, and in 1906 began construction of the Quartz Hill Railroad to deliver the flux to the ore bins at Quartz. By 1915, the Quartz Hill deposits were almost depleted, but shipments continued to Cuargo until 1923. Some mines, such as the Reid, continued to produce flux for the Shasta Zinc & Copper Smelter at Bully Hill until 1927, by which time most mines in the Buckeye area were closed.

A couple is seen sitting on a quartz outcropping at Quartz Hill. The mass of exposed white quartz was described as a beacon for early settlers. The hill was originally prospected for gold but was more profitable as a flux in the copper-smelting process. (Courtesy of Ralph Hollibaugh.)

This photograph is titled "lower tunnel at Quartz Hill Mine" and probably dates from the 1870s, as the rail for the ore carts appears to be wooden. Quartz Hill City was founded early in the Gold Rush when the area known as Buckeye was prospected for placer deposits. The settlement took its name from the large white quartz outcropping seen above. In the 1860s, gold veins were discovered in the quartz, and small lode mines began to work the hill. (Courtesy of Ralph Hollibaugh.)

This photograph at the Quartz Hill Mine is titled "Glory Hole." In 1893, Modest Maryanski incorporated the Original Quartz Hill Gold Mining Company but was often at odds over his transportation route and accidents. Maryanski was denied a permit to build a railroad, but in 1904, the Mammoth Copper Mining Company began buying Maryanski's ore at $2 a ton to use as flux in the copper-smelting process. By 1905, Mammoth Copper was leasing the Quartz Hill property, and by December 1906 began construction of a 3.5-mile railroad to connect Quartz Hill to ore bunkers on the Southern Pacific track at Quartz. The miners appear to be using the block-caving method to collapse ore into a tunnel. When enough ore is removed, the ground surface collapses into a surface depression called a glory hole. In 1915, the ready supply of quartz ore at Quartz Hill was exhausted, and Mammoth Copper began shipping in quartz from Nevada. (Courtesy of Ralph Hollibaugh.)

A train crew of the Quartz Hill Railroad waits as ore is loaded from bins at Quartz Hill. When operations began in 1907, the Mammoth Copper Mining Company purchased a 15-ton Porter engine, as the 3.5-mile route climbed little more than 200 feet in its run from the Sacramento River to the mine. Within eight months, a second, heavier engine was purchased. (Courtesy of Ralph Hollibaugh.)

The Quartz Hill Railroad had to cross the Sacramento River at Spur 27 to load flux ore into ore bins at Quartz (Cuargo) for transfer to the Southern Pacific Railroad for transport to the smelter. The bridge consisted of two 70-foot steel sections of Warren deck truss spans. Over the seven-year period the Quartz Hill Railroad was active, it is estimated that 300,000 tons of flux were transported for use at the smelters. This photograph appears to show the ore bins at Cuargo at center right. (Courtesy of Ralph Hollibaugh.)

This photograph shows the mining crew at Quartz Hill in 1915, when they had almost exhausted the available quartz flux, bringing about the closure of the Quartz Hill Railroad. The heavy Porter engine and the ore cars were sold to the Nevada Short Line Railroad, and the tracks and other material were sold for scrap. (Courtesy of Ralph Hollibaugh.)

The main shaft and ore bunker at the Quartz Hill Mine are shown in this photograph. The loading crew is posing on the middle of the ore bunker. (Courtesy of Ralph Hollibaugh.)

An engine and ore cars are pictured along the route of the Quartz Hill Railroad. The Quartz Hill and Iron Mountain Railroads were narrow gauge. The Southern Pacific and Sacramento Valley & Eastern Railroads utilized standard gauge, which is more expensive to construct but allows for higher speed and capacity. (Courtesy of Ralph Hollibaugh.)

This photograph, taken in the late 1890s, shows the Quartz Hill baseball team in the front and the Bella Vista team in the second row. The inscription on the reverse identifies the man at left in a suit as Frank Hiatt and the man to the right of the bats as Robert "Bob" Hiatt. Frank followed the Klondike Gold Rush to Alaska in 1898. Bob was the son of William T. Hiatt, and both mined in Buckeye for decades. (Courtesy of Ralph Hollibaugh.)

This is a blacksmith shop at Quartz Hill around 1908. The area surrounding Quartz Hill was initially settled for gold mining, but quickly developed a diversified economy that supported a moderate population. Many of the residents, such as the Hiatt family, benefited from the well-paying jobs at the local mines, smelters, and railroads. As the mines and smelters began to close, especially after World War I, many of the locals transitioned back into farming and ranching and continued to reside in Shasta County. (Courtesy of Ralph Hollibaugh.)

The Whitehouse Post Office was established in 1893 in the Old Diggings Mining District and served a group of mines, including the Central, Evening Star, Kit Carson, and Walker Mines. The post office was one mile south of Hart and five miles northeast of Redding, and was named for Whitehouse & Bliss, a mining company that owned the nearby Central Mine. The letter shown here was mailed by the first postmaster Alfred A. Anthony, who was also a developer of the Central Mine, to William O. Blodgett, Shasta County clerk from 1898 until 1906. The post office was closed in 1906 but reopened in 1907 and continued until 1933, when operations were moved to Redding. In 1890, ore from the Central Mine was moved by cable tram to the Central Mine Spur of the Southern Pacific on the west side of the Sacramento River. In 1891, the spur name was changed to simply Central Mine, and the spur was dropped from operation in 1950. (Courtesy of Ralph Hollibaugh.)

This photograph is titled "ore bunkers at Cuargo," a railroad spur between Keswick and Matheson. The Southern Pacific Railroad car is being loaded with quartz flux. By 1880, the Calumet Mines were operating a tramway to the Sacramento River, where its stamp mill was located. In 1890, a railroad spur was opened at Central Mine Spur to ship ore primarily from the Central and Texas Consolidated Mines. In 1907, a second spur was established about two miles away and named Quartz to ship ore from the Quartz Hill property to the Mammoth smelter. In 1908, Quartz was renamed Cuargo and remained in operation until 1923. The Central Mine Spur remained in operation until 1950. (Courtesy of Shasta Historical Society.)

A group of miners pose at the Mammoth Mine in Old Diggings. In the background, just behind the ore cart, is the adit. Even when electricity became available, small mines such as this continued to move ore out of the mines manually. (Courtesy of Ralph Hollibaugh.)

118

These miners are at the adit to the Mammoth Mine in Old Diggings (not to be confused with the mine of the same name at Kennett). The Mammoth Mine was a gold lode mine active in the 1860s that sat idle for a long time. In the 1890s, the mine became active again as a gold mine but later was leased by the United States Smelting, Refining, and Mining Company to supply flux for the smelter at Kennett. (Courtesy of Ralph Hollibaugh.)

The mining crew seen here is from the Reid Mine, which was the principal gold producer in the Old Diggings district. From 1904 until the smelter closed in 1919, the ore was shipped to the Mammoth Copper Company smelter at Kennett. The mine had a reprieve in 1922 when it furnished quartz ore for flux to the Shasta Zinc & Copper Company smelter at Bully Hill. In 1939, dump ore was treated in a flotation plant, but the returns were insufficient to maintain the operation. (Courtesy of Ralph Hollibaugh.)

This photograph shows miners gathered at Old Diggings. The Old Diggings Post Office was founded in 1918 and operated until 1927, when many of the local mines were actively producing copper flux. The post office was near the old Hart Post Office, which operated from 1891 to 1900. The post office takes its name from the Old Diggings Mining District. The mines were actively mined for gold and silver in the 1850s to 1860s and then became idle. When the area again became active in the 1880s, many of the earlier mines were reopened, thus giving the district its name. (Courtesy of Ralph Hollibaugh.)

The Mammoth Quartz Mining Company was organized in 1863 as a gold-mining company in Old Diggings (Quartz Hill). The mine is often confused with the Mammoth Copper Company of Kennett, and there was a connection. In 1904, the United States Smelting, Refining, and Mining Company acquired the Mammoth group near Kennett and formed the Mammoth Copper Mining Company. After the smelter was built in Kennett, the Mammoth Copper Mining Company leased Quartz Hill, which included the Mammoth Mine, to produce quartz for the smelter. (Courtesy of Ralph Hollibaugh.)

This postcard shows the footbridge across the Sacramento River that connected Old Diggings to the Southern Pacific Railroad. The Sacramento River is shown at the peak of dry season; during the winter and spring, the river would have threatened this and other bridge crossings. Transportation was always a problem at many mines, but the footbridge gave residents access to the Southern Pacific's frequent commuter trains. It was common to take the southbound train to Redding in the morning, shop, visit doctors, or do other activities, and then return home on the northbound train. (Courtesy of Ralph Hollibaugh.)

This photograph was taken at the school at Old Diggings in 1895, when the school year was from January to September. The schoolteacher on the left holding a bell is A.F. Souza, who later served as a tax collector and treasurer for the city of Redding. (Courtesy of Shasta Historical Society.)

This photograph is labeled "the Old Hart Mill on the Sacramento River in Old Diggings," but is more correctly the Texas Consolidated Mill at Hart. The mine, which is at the 1,800-foot level to the right, initially was a producer of gold and silver but later produced some low-grade copper ore. The reduction plant at the mill was served by electricity from the Northern California Power Company and consisted of a 20-stamp mill, eight concentrators, and a chlorination plant. The Texas Consolidated Mine, owned by Richard G. Hart Sr., became productive in 1890 as a gold mine; quickly, a small community grew up on the east side of the Sacramento River about seven miles northeast of Redding. The small settlement was also known as Hart's Camp and Hart Village. The Hart Post Office was established in 1891 and named for Richard Hart. The post office operations were moved to the nearby Whitehouse Post Office in 1900, although the Texas Consolidated Mine continued small production into the 1920s. (Courtesy of Ralph Hollibaugh.)

Seven

CENTRAL VALLEY PROJECT AND SHASTA DAM

END OF THE COPPER BOOM

Between 1896 and 1907, six copper and iron smelters were built in the East and West Shasta Copper-Zinc Districts. The smelters brought great wealth to Shasta County and were lauded for creating work, but the complex sulfide ore that long frustrated those seeking gold and silver again created new environmental problems. By 1899, there were fish kills in the Sacramento River below the smelters, and sulfur dioxide fumes began killing orchards and crops from Happy Valley to Cottonwood. The courts were at first heavily on the side of industrialists but slowly swung toward supporting the farmers and began closing the smelters, beginning at Keswick in 1907. Copper was still in demand until the end of World War I, when lower prices, higher shipping costs, and increased legal costs saw the copper boom end. There were holdouts like the zinc operation at Bully Hill, but by 1927, the East and West Copper-Zinc Districts were quiet except for the Mountain Copper Company's sulfide operation at Matheson. The deforestation from logging and the herbicidal effects of sulfur dioxide left the districts with pockets of barren land, which led to erosion that contributed to local flooding. The state finally jumped to action to address the water crisis in 1933 during the Great Depression, when what became known as the Central Valley Project was enacted. The project was to be funded by bonds, but insufficient sales led to the federal government taking over the project as part of its public works program. The Civilian Conservation Corps at camps like Baird started clearing debris behind the site selected for Shasta Dam and putting in reforestation and erosion control steps throughout the copper district. Even before the ground-breaking ceremony at the dam site in September 1937, it was inevitable that many of Shasta County's copper-mining towns would be inundated or bypassed due to the necessity of rerouting the Southern Pacific Railroad's Shasta Route and rerouting of Highway 99 (now Interstate 5). Construction of the dam doomed Winnemum Wintu sites and decades of mining and railroad history, but the influx of workers once again seeking steady employment and good wages created economic recovery and scores of new "boom" towns.

Smoke from the Keswick smelter is seen here. With the other smelters and roasters working, many towns were in a constant fog. The smoke produced by the smelters and the roasting of ore contained such a high sulfur dioxide content that it killed crops and orchards as far south as Cottonwood and remained in the soil for decades. (Courtesy of Shasta Historical Society.)

Deforestation and erosion at Keswick are seen in this 1923 photograph. Caused by the demand for wood for the roasting process and the effects of sulfur dioxide smoke, the denuded hills then became the subject of erosion and increased runoff that in turn brought increased flooding. (Courtesy of Shasta Historical Society.)

As erosion and increased runoff occurred, flooding such as this along the McCloud River at Baird occurred more frequently, often interfering with construction at Shasta Dam and construction of the new railroad route. Severe flooding occurred during the winter of 1936–1937, 1938, and 1940. (Courtesy of Ralph Hollibaugh.)

This view looks downstream at the Sacramento River to the site the engineers selected to anchor the abutments for Shasta Dam. After selection, the Civilian Conservation Corps began clearing the remaining brush and trees, which lasted until World War II stopped the process along the Pit arm of Lake Shasta. The Southern Pacific Railroad had completed its survey for moving the tracks running along the Sacramento River west bank in 1935. By May 1942, the tracks were abandoned for a new route using O'Brien summit, to the left of this photograph (east of the Sacramento River). (Courtesy of Shasta Historical Society.)

This photograph shows a crew rerouting the railroad during the construction of Shasta Dam. In 1935, Southern Pacific engineers completed a survey of the new route that moved the tracks from the west bank of the Sacramento River to the east side by way of a new Pit River Bridge. The new route started at the junction of the Keswick Bridge and climbed to 1,220 feet at the head of O'Brien Creek before descending to Delta. The first passenger train was diverted to the new line on March 17, 1942. (Courtesy of Shasta Historical Society.)

The new Pit River Bridge, shown here under construction, opened in 1942 and served the railroad underneath and what was then Highway 99 above (now Interstate 5). The new bridge was 3,588 feet long and 500 feet above the junction of the McCloud and Pit Rivers. (Courtesy of Shasta Historical Society.)

The water of Lake Shasta can be seen here entering Kennett about 1943. The Kennett Post Office is on the left. The rising lake waters covered the visual evidence of decades of mining and railroad history. (Courtesy of Shasta Historical Society.)

This image shows Shasta Lake in 1948 as the water neared capacity. In 1938, the US government had ordered the removal or destruction of all remaining buildings in the area to be flooded, but World War II impeded completion. Today, the pine trees and chaparral hide remnants of Bully Hill, the iron mine at Heroult, and other mining sites. Iron Mountain, with its huge reddish scar on the ridge, to the west of Redding and Lake Shasta, as well as a few other tailing scars, are all that are readily discernible of the Shasta Copper towns. Most visitors to Lake Shasta, Shasta Caverns, or Shasta Dam see a pristine environment so different from the period between 1890 and 1940. Hopefully, new visitors will be able to see both beauty and history. (Courtesy of Shasta Historical Society.)

DISCOVER THOUSANDS OF LOCAL HISTORY BOOKS
FEATURING MILLIONS OF VINTAGE IMAGES

Arcadia Publishing, the leading local history publisher in the United States, is committed to making history accessible and meaningful through publishing books that celebrate and preserve the heritage of America's people and places.

Find more books like this at
www.arcadiapublishing.com

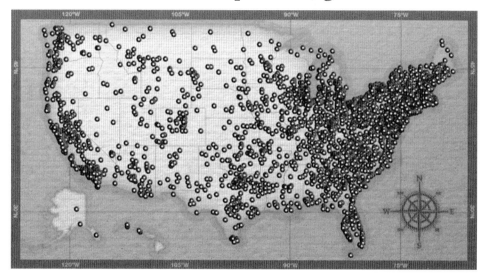

Search for your hometown history, your old stomping grounds, and even your favorite sports team.

Consistent with our mission to preserve history on a local level, this book was printed in South Carolina on American-made paper and manufactured entirely in the United States. Products carrying the accredited Forest Stewardship Council (FSC) label are printed on 100 percent FSC-certified paper.

MADE IN THE USA